THAT PIRATE, BOUCHARD

Revolutions, Redemption and the Plunder of Old California

Also by the Author

BADASS LAWMAN: Guns, Gangs and the Sheriff Who Tamed the Golden State (2022)

THAT PIRATE, BOUCHARD

Revolutions, Redemption and the Plunder of Old California

William Briggs

Published by
William Briggs
Morgan Hill, CA 95037
4943_6

ISBN 978-1-956785-38-8

For Owen, Will and Emma

Table of Contents

Canada (Great Britain)
United States
•Fort Ross - Russia
•San Francisco
•Monterey
•Santa Barbara
•SanJuan Capistrano
Louisiana Territory (France)
New Spain
Mexico City•
Acapulco •
Saint Domingue (France)
Realejo •
New Granada
Equator
Galapagos Islands
Guayaquil •
Brazil (Portugal)
Lima
Callao
Peru
Rio de la Plata
Santiago
•Montevideo
Buenos Aires
Valparaiso•
VICEROYALTIES OF SPANISH AMERICA
C. 1800
Cape Horn

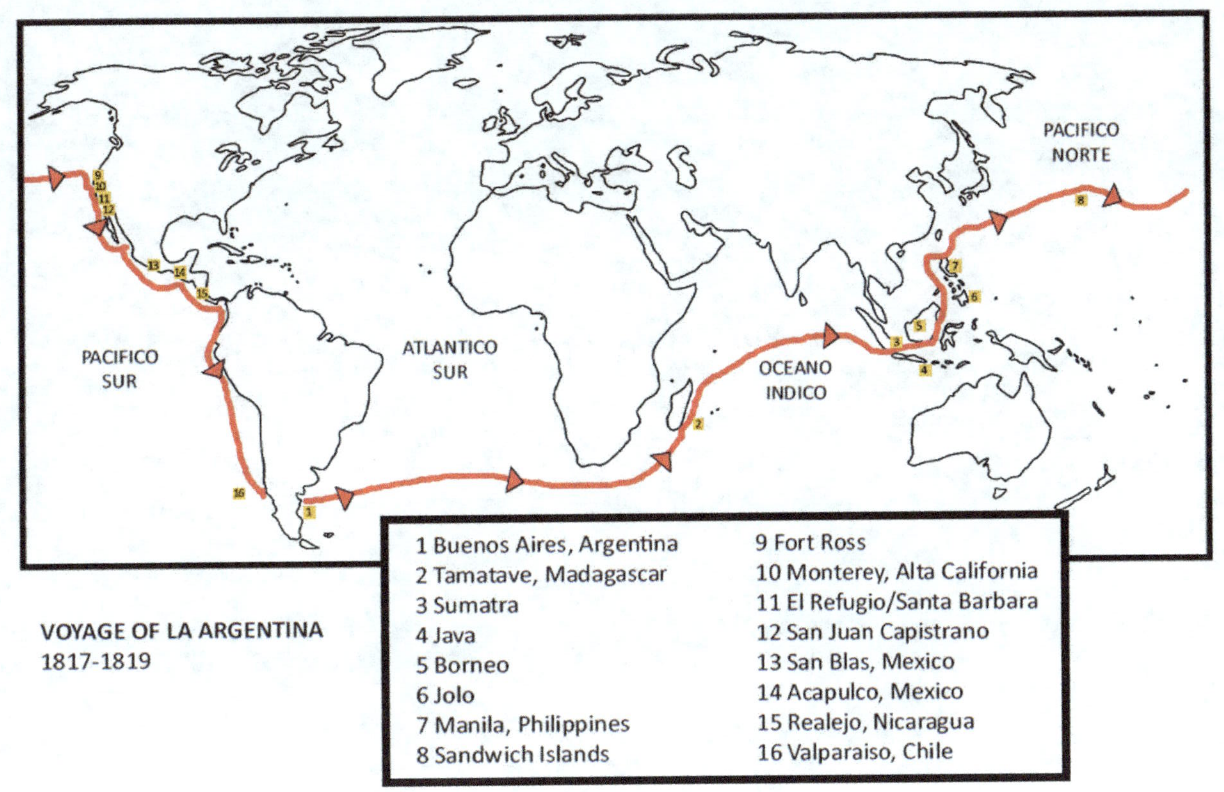

VOYAGE OF LA ARGENTINA
1817-1819

Foreword

After three centuries of European colonization, revolutions of independence changed the political geography of North and South America permanently. American students of history are familiar with our own colonies' break from Great Britain. Less well-known is the story of the wars of independence from Spain in Mexico, Central and South America and the adventures of the Frenchman-turned-Argentine privateer Hypolite Bouchard.

After being granted by the government of Provincias Unidas del Rio de la Plata the authority to serve as a privateer, Commodore Bouchard left the Port of Buenos Aires with the mission of robbing the wealth of Spanish vessels or other sources of bounty. After eighteen months, Bouchard had little to show except for almost circumnavigating the globe, which only a select group of mariners had done. In 1818, with only a little time remaining on his privateer letter, Bouchard sailed to Alta California, where he hoped to finally score the fortune that so far had evaded him. Ultimately, Bouchard returned to South America, claiming his actions aided the struggle of the South American regions to break free from Spain. However, to the *Californios* and other peoples of New Spain, he was simply a *corsario,* a pirate. Undoubtedly, Hypolite Bouchard was an incredibly capable mariner, yet he was also a very complicated individual with all kinds of contradictions.

Professor William Briggs' work on the life and journey of Bouchard is very interesting to read. In the story, he reveals that Bouchard had an extremely complex personality. Bouchard was a child of the French Revolution and a believer in Equality, Liberty and Fraternity, and yet, because of his love of the sea, he, an avowed antimonarchist, was quite willing to serve Emperor Napoleon Bonaparte during his attempt to carve out a European Empire. According to Professor Briggs, it was ironic that Bouchard, who opposed slavery, participated in the French attempt to crush the

Black slave revolt in Haiti. However, after seeing the incredible number of French casualties and sensing the futility of continuing the war against the emancipated Black population of Haiti, Bouchard set sail for South America where he hoped to join the *Americanos'* movement for independence from Spain.

Professor Briggs claims that many intellectuals across the Spanish colonies were engaged in deep discussions and debates on the ideals if the French Revolution and how they could use these ideals to secure the independence of their homelands – their *Patrias Chicas*. Bouchard, on the other hand, neither engaged in profound intellectual discussions about the meaning of equality, liberty and independence, nor thought much about what it meant to free Argentina and the other Spanish colonies on the continent from Spanish rule. Bouchard, a man of action, preferred to be practical. He offered his services as a mariner to the government of Provincias Unidas and also served as a gallant soldier in the army of Jose de San Martin, returning to Buenos Aires to resume his mariner profession before San Martin made his famous crossing of the Andes to liberate Chile.

According to Professor Briggs, Bouchard married the daughter of a wealthy family and used his influence to access Provincias Unidas government officials. He saw no contradiction between serving the cause of independence and earning a respectable income. He offered his services to emerging South American nations in building naval forces, but often found himself serving under preferred British officers such as William Brown in Argentina or Lord Thomas Cochrane in Chile. In 1817, Bouchard received a privateer commission from the Government of Rio de la Plata. Unfortunately, when he and his crew left the port of Buenos Aires and headed eastward, they did not find the wealth-laden Spanish Galleons – no gold or silver nor the expensive silk, spices, or ceramics coming out of China. Professor Briggs observes that it was not until the Bouchard ships reached Central America and northern South America that they ran into Spanish ships and wealthy seaports. But that wealth was not sufficient to pay his officers, crews and creditors in Buenos Aires and Bouchard remained in Chile rather than return to Argentina and his family. Later, the Peruvian government officials rewarded him with haciendas for his work on behalf of the Independence movement and he became a slave owner.

Professor Briggs also observes that Commodore Bouchard was often brutal in his treatment of other human beings. Although opposing slavery, he had gone to Haiti in the French effort to smother the enslaved Black former slaves. He repeatedly abused and mistreated his sailors in the name of discipline during his journey around the globe. He survived assassination attempts and ordered execution of mutineers for treason. It is hard to see him as a person who sincerely valued Liberty, Equality and Fraternity. Ironically, Professor Briggs ends Bouchard's story by telling readers that he was killed by the enslaved people of his Peruvian haciendas when they revolted against his abuse and mistreatment of them. Considering his cruel and brutal ways, one wonders why Bouchard still is so beloved in South America that they have named schools and public places after him.

Nevertheless, Hypolite Bouchard earned his place in South American history and with his pirate raids, in the history of Alta California as well. Professor Briggs' well-researched *That Pirate Bouchard* brings that story to life.

Gregorio Mora Torres Ph.D.
Professor Emeritus, Chicana and Chicano Studies
San Jose State University

Preface

In Argentina, Hipolito Bouchard is revered as a patriot and great naval hero of the wars of independence from Spain. Mostly forgotten today in California, to the Spanish settlers of Alta California, however, he was the scourge from the sea. *El corsario.* ***That pirate Bouchard.*** (***Corsario, el***; Spanish. Masc. noun. From French C*orsaire* [kor ser]. Privateer, a person or ship.)

In the classroom, it was often a useful teaching method to start by defining terms. This is a true story about a *corsario,* the French-born, Argentine privateer Hipolito Bouchard who terrorized Spanish Alta California in the beginning of the 19th century and launched the only pirate raid in California history.

But wait. Did I just use "privateer" and "pirate" in the same description? Indeed, I did. In modern use, the terms are often interchangeable. But there are some distinctions that may remove the semantic ambiguity, though not the ambiguity surrounding Bouchard himself.

The generic term pirate refers to anyone who commits piracy, that is thievery or criminal behavior against another ship on the high seas, or against a coastal location by seaborn attack. A privateer, on the other hand, is a person licensed by a sovereign government to commit acts of piracy against a specific enemy nation's ship or location. Sometimes pirates also operated unofficially on behalf of a government and sometimes privateers attacked ships other than those officially targeted. In other words, the legitimacy of privateering and the criminality of piracy often overlapped. And, of course, one nation's privateer was another nation's pirate. This blurring of the distinction between the two terms plays a central role in the career of Hipolito Bouchard.

Further compounding the confusion is the additional use of other terms such as corsair, freebooter or buccaneer. Corsairs (*corsarios* in Spanish) originally referred to European, Christian sea-bandits in the Mediterranean Sea, such as the Knights of St. John from Malta, who engaged with their North African Muslim counterparts. By the 19th century, the term *corsario* was used to describe privateers anywhere in the Spanish-speaking world. Buccaneers were originally French pirates operating in the Caribbean Sea and along the coast of the Americas. The word derived from *boucon,* a grill for barbequing meat on the island of Hispaniola (modern Haiti and Dominican Republic) which they used as a base to raid rival Spanish shipping and colonies. Over time, *buccaneer* became generic as well. Our narrative will generally use the term privateer, though it will also occasionally employ *pirate* and *corsario.*

Who can resist a good pirate story? Ever since Captain Charles Johnson published *A general History of the Robberies and Murders of the most notorious pirates* in 1724, people have been drawn to tales of adventure on the Spanish Main. *Robinson Crusoe,* by Daniel Defoe (1719) and R.L. Stevenson's *Treasure Island (*1883) have transcended into literary classics. Peter Pan by Sir J.M. Barrie has enchanted generations of children and their parents (who won't grow up) since 1904. The pirate genre has been adapted to countless stage, film, television, video game, music, advertising and sports team applications. People still flock to Gilbert & Sullivan's operetta, *Pirates of Penzance (*1880). Among my all-time favorite movies are *Captain Blood (*1935) and *The Sea Hawk* (1940), both starring Errol Flynn. Robert Newton's turn as Long John Silver in the 1950 production of *Treasure Island* is indelible. Witness the global impact of the *Pirates of the Caribbean* five film franchise, based upon a Disney theme park ride.

A note about the text. This is a work of history, not historical fiction. Any dramatization is simply to propel the narrative along and adheres to the historical record as closely as possible. Any dialogue is actual. Any excesses of creativity are solely my responsibility. Several words in the text are in the Spanish language. They are italicized and at least initially translated. Hopefully they add color and authenticity rather than become an obstacle to the reader. Other Spanish words such as proper nouns for names of places and people, having been appropriated into English in their original form, require no further highlighting. Ships' names are italicized and retain their original Spanish or French or English names. In the 21st century, certain terms of identifying persons or groups, such as Indians, slaves, Negroes (or worse) etc., have been replaced by more sensitive terms such as indigenous people, Native Americans, African Americans, enslaved persons of color. When the former words appear, it represents their early 19th century context and usage, with no intended disrespect. We acknowledge Americans as anyone from either American continent, not just the United States. A pair of maps accompany the text to help readers follow the global sweep of the story and a glossary of sailing ship types and nautical terms follows the story.

Any reader interested in full immersion into adventure upon a 19th century sailing ship, combined with a first-person account of daily life in Mexican California, should look at the classic *Two Years Before the Mast,* by Richard Henry Dana, Jr. (1840). And if you haven't cracked Herman Melville's *Moby Dick* since high school, it's time to revisit this masterpiece of the sea.

With a deep passion for less well-known stories from California's unique and colorful history, I was intrigued from the beginning about the notion of pirates in California. The locales in California (Fort Ross, Monterey, Santa Barbara, San Juan Capistrano) were all familiar to me; the pirate connection was not. With research, the story opened to an epic tale as broad as the Pacific Ocean, tying California to the less-known struggle of the Spanish colonies of America for independence, with characters every bit as compelling as in our own nation, fighting for a cause as great as the one our own colonial patriot founding fathers fought for. A harsh and complicated man, Hipolito Bouchard was often his own worst enemy. He was an idealist, a patriot, a privateer, and perhaps a pirate. So, hoist that mainsail, unfurl the topgallants and come aboard with *"that pirate Bouchard" to r*elive that period in history when he sought out the Spanish on the high seas and the pale blue and white flag of Argentina briefly flew over California.

William Briggs
Morgan Hill, California
2023

Introduction

"It's more fun to be a pirate than to join the navy."

–Steve Jobs

For as long as there have been sea travel and commerce there has been piracy. It is a global phenomenon. Early Phoenicians were plagued by pirates in the Aegean and Adriatic seas. Julius Caesar was famously kidnapped by pirates. My Viking ancestors who sailed their longships out from Scandinavia as far as North America centuries before Columbus and raided from Russia to Ireland were pirates as well as great navigators. As the era of exploration dawned by the 15th century, trade increased dramatically and so did those preying upon trade routes. As global trade evolved and nations began to acquire overseas colonies, few had the means to establish a navy capable of protecting those assets. There had always been willing mercenaries to fight countries' land battles and countries also turned to privateers to supplement their naval force. Privateers would supply, outfit, arm and crew their own ships at their own expense, being granted a governmental letter of marque, formally authorizing the privateer to attack enemy ships. The recovered booty – ships, cargo, treasure, even crew or slaves – would be divided among the investors, the ship's crew and the government. The risks were often great, but so were the potential rewards all around. It was legalized piracy.

Among the many famous privateers were the English Martin Frobisher (b. 1535) who made three voyages searching for the Northwest Passage to Asia; Henry Morgan, (b. 1635) the Welshman who ravaged Panama and became lieutenant governor of Jamaica; Captain William Kidd (b. c. 1645), the Scotsman who supposedly left an enormous buried treasure and was executed for piracy; and Jean Lafitte (b. c. 1780), the Frenchman who plied the Gulf of

Mexico and helped the Americans win the Battle of New Orleans in the Second British War (1812-14).

The most famous privateer of all, and the most significant to California history, was Francis Drake. Drake, along with his second cousin John Hawkins (1532), were English naval commanders. Drake was the first sailor to survive a voyage around the globe. Both men were largely responsible for the defeat of the Spanish Armada (1588) and had held commissions from Queen Elizabeth I to plunder Spanish ships and maintain English dominance of the seas. They were known as the *Sea Dogs* and knighted by the Queen. (As his direct descendant, this author was chagrined to learn that John Hawkins also established the lucrative triangle slave trade between England, West Africa and the Americas.)

England lagged behind Spain and Portugal in building an overseas colonial empire in the 16th century. In 1578, Drake followed in the wake of Ferdinand Magellan and sailed his ship, the *Golden Hind,* into the Pacific Ocean, where he looted Spanish-held ports and captured Spanish shipping, before returning to England with several tons of gold, silver, coins and treasure taken from England's enemy. His subsequent successes against Spain enabled England to become a global naval superpower and assured his fame and fortune.

Enroute, Drake had sailed north along the west coast of both American continents, searching for a northern passage back to England. At some point Drake anchored off the California coast to repair his ship, interacted with local Miwok Native Americans, and claimed the land he called Nova Albion for England. Historians have long debated the exact location of Drake's landing. Most concur it was somewhere north of the entrance to San Francisco Bay, most likely the Point Reyes peninsula and today's Drake's Bay. Some modern researchers, however, contend that his landfall was farther north near the present Oregon border.[1] In any event, his mission was considered a state secret and details were not released for decades. Drake adds English antecedents to California's "discovery" stories.

During the North American colonial war for independence, Britannia's Royal Navy ruled the waves. The colonies had no way to match its strength. However, no less than George Washington, himself, recognized the need for a naval force to augment his troops ashore and he lobbied the Continental Congress to provide for its establishment. Lacking sufficient resources to underwrite a large navy, in March 1776, Congress began commissioning privateers to harass British shipping. The use and scale of privateers grew steadily as the war dragged on.

There was one problem with the dependence upon privateers: despite its risks, which included capture and impressment into the British Navy, it was lucrative enough to lure able seamen away from enlisting in the nascent American Navy. According to historian and admiral Samuel Eliot Morrison, prize money was extremely important to sailors, naval or civilian, during the 18th century and the imbalance between Navy pay and shares of the capture of an enemy vessel and that divided among privateers was enough for John Paul Jones, called the Father of the American Navy, to write:

> *"[Unless] the private Emoluments of individuals in our Navy is made superior to that in Privateers it (the Navy) can never become respectable – it never will become formandable (sic). And without a Respectable Navy – alas America!"*[2]

Congress did respond and adjust the division of spoils. Nevertheless, by the end of the Revolutionary War, more than 800 privateer ships had been commissioned and they had captured or destroyed more than 600 British ships, as well as transporting valuable supplies to the colonies.[3]

As a sovereign nation following independence, United States ships no longer enjoyed the protection of either the British or French fleets. Shipping to important ports in the Mediterranean, as well as Atlantic Iberia and West Africa, was easy prey to Barbary pirates from North Africa (Tunis, Tripoli, Algiers and Morocco) who demanded huge extortion payments from foreign merchant fleets. These Muslim pirates were privateers with a different set of rules, believing all shipping from non-Islamic nations to be fair game. With a depleted treasury from the war debt and no navy to protect the trade, President Thomas Jefferson resorted to military force, sending the Marines to North Africa, hence the lyrics *"To the shores of Tripoli"* in the Marine Corps hymn.

Although Great Britain lost a sizeable piece of its empire as a result of America's successful revolution, it nevertheless still retained its military might and mastery of the seas. With horror, Britain watched another revolution unfold across the English Channel with the destruction of the French monarchy and the Reign of Terror. In France, another military power was soon preparing to challenge Britain's dominance under the charismatic leadership of Napoleon Bonaparte. And into the maw of Napoleonic ambition would be drawn a young Frenchman named Andre-Paul Bouchard.

This, then, is the story of Andre-Paul Bouchard, who would rise from young French seaman in Napoleon's campaigns in Egypt and Malta, to participate in the abortive attempts to crush the Haitian slave revolt and then transfer his idealism from France to the struggle of the Spanish colonies in South America to remove the yoke of Spain and become independent. Bouchard would prove his mettle as both a soldier and a sailor in the service of the fledgling Argentina. He would also play a role in Jose de San Martin's liberation of Chile and Peru. In the process he would be granted letters of marque to challenge arch-enemy Spain on the high seas and he would sail around the globe searching for Spanish plunder and fighting for Argentine independence. His extraordinary voyage would sail him to the slave dens of Madagascar, the pirate strongholds of Indonesia, the blockade of Manila Bay, and the Polynesian court of the Hawaiian king. All this before he set his sights on the remote outpost of Spanish Empire, Alta California. For a month, in the fall of 1818, Hipolito Bouchard (curiously he had adopted his brother's first name) terrorized the *presidios* and missions of Old California – the only pirate raid and land-sea battle ever waged in California. Then he sailed away. Arriving in the friendly country of Chile he expected a hero's welcome; instead, he found himself arrested for piracy. Exonerated but humiliated and impoverished, he sought redemption in aiding *el Libertador* Simon Bolivar's push to liberate Peru.

Following the Crimean War in 1856, the community of nations agreed to forbid seizing enemy goods on neutral ships or neutral countries' goods on enemy ships. Also eliminated was the issuance of letters of marque. Thus, in the twilight of the Age of Sail, the privateers of history sailed away forever.[4] (However, piracy remains alive in the 21st century in the waters off the Somali coast, the Straits of Malacca and elsewhere). Nevertheless, during the Spanish wars of liberation, privateers played a very important role, and none more than Hipolito Bouchard. Mid-way though his circumnavigation of the globe he sailed toward the California coast of North America, and we start his story there.

Notes:

1. Andrew Lawler, "Did Francis Drake Really Land in California?" https://www.smithsonainmag.com>history>did-francis-drake-really-land-in-california, retrieved June 23, 2022.

2. Samuel Eliot Morison, John Paul Jones. A Sailors Biography. Boston: Little Brown & Co., 1959, pp. 66-69.

3. John Frayler, *Privateers in the American Revolution,* National Park Service, https://www.nps.gov>articles. Retrieved June 24, 2022.

4. Gerardo Diaz Flores, *What is the Difference Between Corsairs and Pirates?,* https://www.relatosehistoriasenmexico, num. 118, (translated) retrieved June 25, 2022.

Chapter 1

Wary Neighbors

"With all sails full, we ran for the harbor. As we neared the fort, we could see a great commotion among the soldiers. When we were abreast of it one of them asked through a speaking trumpet: 'What ship is that?' 'Russian!', we replied."

–Nikolai Rezanov, in a letter to the Russian Minister of Commerce at Archangel, July 17, 1806, describing his entry into San Francisco Bay, Alta California

"Inside the said square they are constructing housing that is well built, and accordingly it demonstrates as stated that they plan to establish themselves there."

–Luis Arguello, reporting to Alta California Governor Arrillaga on the Russians establishing Fort Ross, September 7, 1812

One morning in November 1818, a Russian lookout peered through his spyglass, through what Sir Francis Drake's chaplain had once called "stinking fogges," squinting to make out the two ships coming from the western horizon toward the rocky Pacific coast of North America. As the ships sailed closer, he couldn't recognize the sky blue and white flag the vessels flew; certainly not the bold red and yellow banner of the neighboring Spaniards, nor did it show the crosses of the British Union Jack. And though he had only seen the stars and stripes of the new American republic a few times on a couple of whalers, it was not that ensign either.

Soon the sentry was joined on the headland by others from the nearby Russian settlement known as Ross Colony, including Ivan

Alexandrovich Kuskov, manager of the agricultural and trading outpost run by the Russian-American Company. By the time the Russians scrambled down the cliff-side path to the rocky shore, an incoming tide was quickly reclaiming the small beach. For lack of any deep-water port, the two frigates had dropped anchor rather than risk sailing too close to the rocky shore and had launched landing parties in a pair of longboats. The Russians watched admiringly as the bronze skinned oarsmen – they appeared to be Polynesians – skillfully crested the rolling shore breakers and rode the surf smoothly into the cove.

As the longboats beached, Kuskov recognized Peter Corney, an English sailor he had met previously. They shook hands and, deferentially, Corney indicated the tall, dark-haired man in a full naval officer uniform stepping from the other longboat. Removing his bi-corn hat, the officer formally bowed and introduced himself, using French as the common language: Captain Hipolito Bouchard, of *las Provincias Unidas del Rio de la Plata* – the Argentine republic – master of the frigate, *la Argentina* and the corvette *Santa Rosa de Chacabucco.*

The Russians eyed the diverse, polyglot crew from the ships: Filipinos, Chinese, Africans, Indonesians as well as the Sandwich Islanders, Europeans and South American *creoles.* Kuskov sensed they were no threat, as Captain Bouchard explained the ships were enroute from the Kingdom of Hawai'i and headed back to South America. He was looking to resupply his ships at Ross Colony on the advice of Peter Corney, his second-in-command, before sailing southward. Carrying letters of marque, his only enemy was Spain, and his only targets were Spanish shipping or Spanish ports-of-call along the California coast.

Ivan Kuskov had a sense of ambivalence about these Argentine privateers. On the one hand, he was a businessman and entrepreneur, willing to trade with anyone. California may have been remote, but it was increasingly on the trade and exploration routes of many nations and the Russians did business with them all. The British had sent Captains James Cook and George Vancouver on a scientific exploration and to search for a northwest passage between the Atlantic and Pacific oceans. The British had designs on the

Oregon territory of the Pacific Northwest dating back centuries to Drake's voyage, although they never made any effort at colonization. French explorer Jean Francois Galaup de La Perouse had plied these waters as well. American Boston Whalers were becoming more common. Since being granted a monopoly on the fur trade in Russian North America in 1799, the Russians, with fewer ships, often contracted to use American ships and crews in their fur hunting forays along the Pacific coast. This increased American presence was early indication of United States westward expansion in the years to come. Ships of many nations sailed from Asia to Hawai'i before touching California and returning to their home ports. The Pacific Ocean was no longer a Spanish lake.

Kuskov's ambivalence was regarding Spain, which had claimed California since the 15th century and colonized it from the 16 hundreds. In order to blunt any foreign incursion, Madrid had ordered the establishment of *presidios* (forts) and a string of Franciscan Catholic missions through the coastal valleys of California. The closest were established only a matter of miles away on San Francisco Bay (Spain would soon build two more missions north of San Francisco closer to the Ross Colony, bringing the total to twenty-one: Mission San Raphael in 1817 and the last in the chain, Mission San Francisco de Solano, constructed in 1823). Thus, Spain and Russia were neighbors. They coexisted as neighbors often do. For their part, the Orthodox Christian Russians laughed at Spanish claims to most of the Western Hemisphere under the Treaty of Tordesillas in 1494, in which the Roman Catholic pope divided up the New World between Spain and Portugal. And the Spaniards in Alta California, including at the missions, were in such need of manufactured goods, that they readily ignored Spain's prohibition against trading with any other nations and engaged hungrily with the Russians. Kuskov didn't want to provoke the Spaniards nor adversely affect his own settlement at Ross, but a further-weakened Spain could only work to the Russians' advantage. He welcomed Captain Bouchard to his headquarters inside the stockade at Ross. As an agent of Imperial Russia, he was also interested in obtaining any intelligence Bouchard might share.

Both Spain and Russia sought to expand their empires by what they believed was divine right. While Spain exploited the Americas,

Russia moved east into vast Siberia. As Spain exploited the gold and silver wealth of Mexico and South America, the Russians found huge wealth in the "soft gold" of fur. In addition to the warmth they provided in frigid climates, pelts from a wide variety of animals, wolf, fox, marten, beaver, became a luxury item signifying wealth. And the most profitable of these furs was the soft, dense pelt of the sea otter. Otter fur brought enormous prices, especially in the markets of Canton, China. The hunt for otter fur brought the expansionist Russians across Siberia to the icy waters of the Bering Sea, Kodiak Island and the North American mainland itself.

According to historian Owen Matthews,

> *"Since the 1780s Russian merchant-adventurers had established a hold – albeit a precarious one – on the Pacific shore of America. A string of lonely stockades and forts manned by a motley array of convicts, fur trappers and foreign desperadoes spanned 4,000 miles of the northern Pacific rim from the Kamchatka peninsula through the Aleutian archipelago to the newly founded capital of Russian America at New Archangel – modern Sitka – at the southern end of the present-day US state of Alaska. Nonetheless {Nikolai} Rezanov was convinced that the unclaimed 1,500 miles of territory that separated New Archangel from San Francisco was ripe for the taking – as was the sparsely populated and barely defended empire of New Spain that lay beyond."*[1]

The first serious plan for the annexation of the North American coast was conceived in 1806 by Nikolai Rezanov, a diplomat and courtier to Empress Catherine the Great. On an exploratory voyage to California, Rezanov realized Russian survival in the area would depend upon trading relations with the Spaniards. Arriving in San Francisco, ill and near starving, aboard the ship *Juno,* he entered negotiations with colonial Governor Jose Joaquin de Arillaga and *comandante* of the San Francisco *presidio* Jose Dario Arguello. The Spanish had been admonished by Madrid to receive the visitors with wary kindness. While there, discussions went so favorably that Rezanov also became engaged to Arguello's teen-aged daughter, Concepcion. Proposing to establish a Russian agricultural outpost in unoccupied land abutting the northern-most Spanish territory, Rezanov returned to Russia to secure imperial support for his plans from the new tsar, having promised to return to his young Spanish *novia* (betrothed). Enroute to St. Petersburg, Rezanov died. However, his plans found support from Alexandr Andreivich Baranov, the Russian governor of Alaska and head of the Russian-American Company. Baranov's deputy, Ivan Kuskov, was soon dispatched on expeditions to locate a site and establish a colony. By 1811, the Russian-American Company had settled above a cove north of the bay originally called Bodega when discovered by Drake and renamed Rumyantsev Bay by the Russians. The actions of the Russians made clear their intentions to remain in Spanish-claimed California.

In an 1808 letter of instruction from Governor Baranov to Ivan Kuskov, he writes,

> *"...above all you are to try, if you have a chance, to establish future mutually advantageous, amicable trade and hunting relations, so we can freely supply them [Spaniards] with our goods in exchange for their products. Do not make sea otters an item of trade, nor take them at any price, until such time as you make the Spanish more inclined to allow our hunting parties to hunt without interference along the coast of California in places where there are most animals and where hunting is more desirerable."*[2]

The outpost on the Sonoma coast was intended to be a trading post, although it resembled a military fort. As a result, by the time California became part of the United States, the site had become known in English as Fort Ross. Today, a reconstructed Fort Ross is the centerpiece of a California State Historic Park. A stockade was constructed from locally sourced redwoods. A two-story blockhouse anchored two of the corners and the fort was well-defended by numerous cannon. Inside, the manager's comfortable house, barracks for company employees and warehouses surrounded an open center, watched over by the two-headed eagle on the imperial flag. Outside the stockade, the Russians maintained a garden for vegetables and planted fruit trees, hoping to export surplus back to often-starving colleagues in Alaska. There were various farm outbuildings and a corral for livestock as well.

The population of the Ross colony varied with an average of a hundred Russians and another hundred Native Alaskans (Aleuts), along with many Kashaya, local Native Americans used as day-labor, and who were generally well-treated. About a year before Bouchard's arrival, the Russians reaffirmed their relationship with the local Native Americans. Chiefs received medals engraved with the likeness of the tsar, acknowledging that the indigenous people had rights to the land the Russians used for commerce. This was in sharp contrast to the Spanish who considered it their Christian and royal duty to claim the lands of others on behalf of their king and church.[3] Few Russian women lived at Ross Colony, however many of the men intermarried with Native Kashaya, Coastal Miwok and Southern Pomo native women in sanctioned unions. Everyone worked for the Russian-American Company; it was a company town.[4]

Captain Bouchard took full advantage of the time at Ross Colony. He refilled his water barrels and took on a supply of fresh produce hoping to forestall any further outbreaks of scurvy. Significantly, he also replenished his ships' store of gunpowder, anticipating – even hoping for – engagement with the Spaniards. His crew ashore enjoyed a brief rest in the garden-like setting, while the crew remaining onboard the ships attended to the never-ending repair needs to rigging and sail. Bouchard, himself, took full advantage of Manager Kuskov's hospitality. Kuskov was a loyal subject of the autocratic Tsar Paul I and was intrigued by this stern man who had once served Russia's archenemy in the Napoleonic navy, then renounced his French allegiance to next serve the cause of South American republicanism. Over cigars and Spanish wine, Kuskov sought any information from the wider world. He was convinced that neither Argentina nor any of the other emerging South American republics had any designs on North America. He inquired about what Bouchard knew of British interests in the Pacific northwest. And he was particularly interested in any news from Hawai'i, since Bouchard had had negotiations with High King Kamehameha at his most recent port of call, where Hawai'i had apparently been the first sovereign nation to recognize the newly created Argentina. It had only been a year since the Russians had backed an abortive coup by the king of Kauai Island against Kamehameha to force concessions and establish a similar Russian settlement in the islands. The venture had ended in disaster and diplomatic humiliation for the Russians.

For his part, Bouchard elicited as much information about Spanish Alta California as he could. Much of the information confirmed earlier reports from Peter Corney: Spain was weakened, the province was sparsely populated and lightly defended. Bouchard also sought Kuskov's opinion about the loyalty of the Alta California people – would they join the hemispheric revolt against their Iberian masters? Factions in Mexico had been in revolt for almost a decade. Kuskov demurred. Revolution would not enter the Russian psyche until a century later. Bouchard consulted Russian maps, asked about ports, tides and weather, and what other national interests might be in the mix. Strangely, Bouchard did not seem particularly interested in Yerba Buena (San Francisco), but rather seemed fixated on the capital at Monterey. His visit to Ross Colony had been brief and efficient, but apparently not of great significance to Bouchard; he failed to mention it in his subsequent report detailing his around-the-world navigation. He simply wrote,

> *"On the 25th of October I sailed from these islands ([Hawai'i] toward the Alta California coast, and on the 22nd of November we anchored in the Bay of Monterey, Capital of Alta California."*[5]

Captain Bouchard and Peter Corney thus rejoined their crews aboard *la Argentina* and *Santa Rosa* and sailed south past the golden gateway entrance into San Francisco Bay on a course for Monterey. The simple truth was that the Spanish had been incapable of preventing the Russian incursion north of San Francisco Bay. And now, despite another ship a few weeks earlier, also out from Hawai'i, that had warned the Spaniards that a privateer squadron was heading their way, there was little either the governor or the missionaries of Alta California could do about that either. Hipolito Bouchard was about to strike a blow for independence against Argentina's enemy and sail into infamy as well.

But his story began almost four decades earlier, in France on the eve of revolution…

Notes:

1. Owen Matthews, Glorious Misadventures: Nikolai Rezanov and the Dream of Russian America, New York: Bloomsbury, 2013, pp. 8-9.

2. Letter from Alexander Baranov to Ivan Kuskov, Oct. 14, 1808, from Basil Dmytryshyn, A.P. Crownhart-Vaughn and Thomas Vaughn, The Russian American Colonies, vol. 3, 1798-1867, Portland: Oregon Historical Press, 1989. Reproduced in Glenn J. Farris ed., So Far From Home. Russians in Early California, Berkeley, CA: Heyday/Santa Clara University, 2012, p.55.

3. Glenn J. Farris, Ibid. p. 74.

4. Stephen Watrous, "Russian Expansion to America," from Fort Ross, Fort Ross Interpretive Association, Fort Ross Conservancy, 1998, https://www.fortross.org>russian-american-company, retrieved June 28, 2022.

5. Hipolito Bouchard, manuscript, Feb. 10, 1819, transcribed and translated in Peter Uhrowczik, The Burning of Monterey – the 1818 Attack on California by the Privateer Bouchard, Los Gatos CA: Cyril Books, 2001. p. 119. The original manuscript is in the Archivo General de la Nacion, Buenos Aires.

Chapter 2
Revolutionary Sailor

"A State can be no better than citizens of which it is composed. Our labour now is not to mold states but to make citizens"

–Voltaire, *Candide*, 1759

"I am sometimes a fox and sometimes a lion. The whole secret of government lies in knowing when to be one or the other."

–Napoleon Bonaparte

"Liberty, equality, fraternity or death; – the last, much easiest to bestow, O Guillotine!"

–Charles Dickens, *A Tale of Two Cities,* 1859

By the final decades of the 18th century Europe was in flux. Like the sudden cold mistral winds of Provence that turned the sky red, winds of change swirled from Madrid to Moscow. Not everyone felt them, but to those who did, they felt ominous. Spain, flabby from centuries of squeezing wealth from its far-flung colonies, had dissipated its treasury in never-ending wars and was losing its grip on its empire. Britain had allowed the unimaginable and, despite its military might, watched its American colonies break away and create – of all things – a republican democracy. (Yet, to his credit, King George III worked with his parliament to enact some reforms that addressed the changing world, and thereby may have lost his colonies but saved his head.) In France the excesses of the long reign of Louis XV (without the sure hand of his predecessor, Louis XIV, the Sun King) were now being passed along to Louis XVI, who was unable to confront change or enact reform – until it was too late. The highly stratified French order, the Three Estates of aristocracy, bourgeoisie, and peasantry, was about to convulse from new evolving social, political and economic ideas. Ideas were becoming as powerful as armies.

Not quite a decade before all these ideas coalesced and then exploded in revolution and the chaos that followed, and nearly four decades before he sailed into Monterey Bay, Hipolito Bouchard was born January 15, 1780, in the French commune of Bormes-les-Mimosas, in the Van Department of Provence-Alpes-Cote d'Azur. His baptismal name, which he would change later, was Andre Paul Bouchard Brunet, named for his father Andre Louis Bouchard. His mother was Anne Marie Therese Brunet. The Bouchards had lived in the Van Department, along the Mediterranean, since the time of his 4x great grandfather Louis Bouchard in the late 16th century, and probably generations before that. Bormes-les-Mimosas was a peaceful hillside commune, a short walk from the sandy beaches of the sea through narrow alleys, the walls covered with magenta colored bougainvillea. Named for the mimosa shrub with its puffy yellow flowers, the perfume of honey and jasmine scented the town's salt air.

Though Bormes-les-Mimosas was idyllic and picturesque, his father soon moved the Bouchard family down the hill to the better opportunities afforded at Saint Tropez, on the Bay of Grimaud, between Nice and Marseille. An important port since medieval times, Saint Tropez, named for a Pisan martyr, bustled with commerce as the produce of Provence, wine, wood and cork, made their way into trade with the wider world. Saint Tropez also had a military presence; a local militia had been formed centuries earlier to repel repeated attacks by Barbary pirates and other sea raiders from across the Mediterranean. Father Bouchard engaged in the cork trade and young Andre-Paul was expected to follow. But Saint Tropez also had an established shipyard and a thriving fishing industry. Here sailors and fishermen told tales of life at sea, and young Bouchard, like his grandfather before him, was drawn to a nautical life.

Although Saint Tropez was far from the Parisian epicenter of the 1789 revolution that swept away the monarchy and reordered French society, it had not been isolated from the myriad radical ideas that gave that era the name Age of Enlightenment. The writings of British libertarians such as John Locke, Thomas Hobbes and David

Hume had circulated widely on the continent, as had the thoughts of the French *philosophes.* French writers and thinkers such as Charles Louis de Secondat-Baron de Montesquieu, Jean-Jacques Rousseau and most particularly Francois-Marie Aroet de Voltaire, the most known and respected (not by all) Frenchman of the 18th century, were discussed, debated and argued about throughout France. And Americans also contributed to the conversation. Not only had America gained independence with French help, but also Benjamin Franklin, the most famous abroad of all Americans, was in residence in the Passy neighborhood of Paris for many years adding wisdom and spice to the intellectual stew. The framers of the French Republic's founding document, *the Declaration of the Rights of Man and the Citizen*, had consulted Thomas Jefferson, lead author of America's *Declaration of Independence,* who was serving as United States Ambassador to France. While the atomic fusion of all this brainpower may not have directly caused the French Revolution, it certainly laid a pathway upon which once taken, there could be no return.

Historian Stanley Hoffmann writes,

> *"The revolt had been staged just at the time when the old bonds had lost any justification, and when the monarchy, precisely because of its own blend of authoritarian and noninterventionist features had managed to lose touch with a changing society, thus forfeiting its usefulness as a common form of reference and appearing increasingly arbitrary."*[1]

The ringing revolutionary ideals of *liberte, egalite, fraternite* that swept France must have had a profound impact on the adolescent Bouchard, particularly the concept of *egalite.* Now Frenchmen would not be predestined to a certain station or occupation. Working class families like his own could aspire to achieve and succeed on their merits. But the Revolution was not without opposition. From abroad, European monarchies shuddered as the guillotine dropped on the necks of Louis XVI and his queen, Marie Antoinette. (Her brother, Emperor of Austria, took particular umbrage; war would follow). England had also experienced regicide a century earlier, but soon restored the monarchy and regained continuity. Restrictions on the French clergy and the church embittered Catholics everywhere. Internally, conservative or reactionary elements challenged the workings of the new French government.

According to John Cairns,

> *"In five years, the country had moved from the ancien regime, through a conservative constitutional settlement characterized by the rule of the well-to-do, to a radical left-wing dictatorship cowing the Convention and ruling without a constitution...Caught between...radical groups on the left and the clerical, royalist, peasant forces on the Right, the Directors were steadily more dependent on the new and powerful army of the Revolution."*[2]

In the end,

> *"Bonaparte was to sum up the striving for unity by putting an end to politics, identifying himself with the will of the nation, and imposing the most highly centralized legal and administrative system, that the French had ever known."*[3]

Originally from Corsica, young Napoleon Bonaparte obtained a scholarship to the French military academy when his island became acquired by France. He was held back from advancement in part by his ethnicity until the revolution reformed the army and he obtained a commission in the artillery. Napoleon first came to national attention during the Siege of Toulon in 1793. Toulon had been an important Mediterranean port city since Provence was integrated into France in the 15th century. It was also the home port of the French Mediterranean fleet. During widespread Federalist revolts in 1793, Toulon revolted against the government of the First Republic and handed the city over to the British navy, actively supporting the counterrevolutionaries. With a third of the French fleet bottled up in Toulon, retaking the port was of vital strategic importance to the revolutionary government, which still had a massive land army under its command. Through his friendship with Augustin de Robespierre, (brother of the violent head of the French revolutionary government,

Maximilien Robespierre), Napoleon was given a command at the besieged city. After four months, the British evacuated, along with their Spanish and royalist French allies. As the British ships lifted their blockade of the port, they destroyed several French ships and fired the warehouses along the docks. More than 14,000 royalists escaped onboard the British ships, and many more were stampeded in the panic or killed by advancing Republican troops. Napoleon was lauded for his aggressive strategic planning and bravery. By the end of the siege in December he had been promoted all the way to brigadier general and was dispatched to Nice to assume artillery command of the Army of Italy.

During the Siege of Toulon, young Andre-Paul Bouchard could watch the artillery flashes knife through the evening clouds from the docks at Saint Tropez, several miles to the east. He might have been able to hear the enormous explosion of the powder magazines when the British torched the ships. Saint Tropez was safely in control of the Republicans, but the local citizenry had nervously followed events at Toulon. With Toulon back in Republican hands, Saint Tropez no doubt celebrated the emergence of a new national hero, Napoleon. And the port at Toulon quickly began repairing the damaged fleet and replacing the two dozen ships that had been destroyed. Meanwhile Bouchard divided his time between formal schooling and hanging around the dockyards, assisting local fishermen. In April 1797, his father died. As eldest son, Bouchard was given more responsibilities. However, when his mother remarried, the stepfamilies did not blend well, and Andre-Paul looked to move away. In 1799, approaching manhood and full of revolutionary zeal, he enlisted in the French navy. For training he was sent to Toulon, attached to the 5th complementary at the school of apprentice gunners.

Not long before nineteen-year-old Bouchard arrived in Toulon to learn the ropes of manning a French naval warship, Napoleon Bonaparte sailed from that same harbor. Following a brilliant campaign in Italy and dictating peace to Austria, the Corsican convinced the Directorate to put off invasion plans of England, and, instead, launch a strike against Egypt, hoping to disrupt British trade and their control of India. Enroute, the French achieved a bloodless capture of Malta, then advanced on Egypt, defeating the Mamluks at

Giza before entering Cairo. Again, Napoleon seemed unstoppable. At sea it would be a different story.

After a summer of hide-and seek with the British Navy, British Admiral Horatio Nelson finally found the French fleet in the Bay of Aboukir, some twenty miles east of Alexandria. In a strong position, backed by an artillery battery on the land behind them, the French admiral choose to fight at anchor. However, Nelson's early arrival surprised the French and, in a battle fought into the night by light of burning ships, the British destroyed eleven French warships, including the flagship *L'Orient,* and two frigates. No British ships were lost. In the wake of the worst naval defeat of the Napoleonic era, Napoleon's plans for invading India went down with the fleet. Only two French frigates and two warships escaped the Battle of the Nile. One was *le Genereux,* which had also previously avoided destruction by the departing British during the siege of Toulon and would soon become seaman Bouchard's first duty call.

With his escape route to sea eliminated, Bonaparte spent several fruitless months campaigning in Egypt and waiting for an opportunity to return to Europe. When a new European coalition appeared to be threatening invasion of France itself, Bonaparte abandoned his Egyptian army in August 1799 and returned to France, where, unaware of the disaster in Egypt, the French welcomed him as a hero and potential savior. By careful political maneuvering, he engineered a new constitution, giving himself virtually unlimited powers as First Consul. The political elite had lost faith in the system they had created, a common fate of weak compromise regimes. To the question, "What's in the new Constitution?" the simple answer was "Bonaparte."[4] It was a bloodless coup. Meanwhile, the British, now in almost total command of the sea were blockading the French garrison on the island of Malta. Considered essential to any naval activity in the Mediterranean, and particularly the long-delayed evacuation of Napoleon's army stranded in Egypt, control of Malta was of strategic importance. Once again, the French would challenge Britain over this island set in the middle of the *middle sea.* And Bouchard would find himself in the middle of it all.

Since the early Middle Ages, Malta had been home to the wealthy chivalric order, the Sovereign Military Hospitaller Order of Saint John of Jerusalem, of Rhodes and of Malta, commonly called the Knights of Malta, with roots back to the Crusades. When Napoleon captured Malta on the way to Egypt, he stripped the Knights of their administrative power and sought to access their treasury. The population of Malta chafed at French occupation. Emboldened by Nelson's victory in Egypt, local Maltese insurgents stepped up a guerilla war against the French. Besieged for many months between Maltese partisans and the British blockading the harbors, the French garrison inside Valletta was rapidly running short of food and suffering from disease. In early February 1800 the French launched a relief effort from Toulon with supplies and some 3,000 reinforcements to aid the starving soldiers on Malta. The squadron consisted of the frigate *Badine,* the corvettes *San Pareille* and *Fauvette,* a transport *Ville de Marseille* and the 74-gun ship of the line *le Genereux.* Among the 700-sailor crew of *le Genereux* was Andre-Paul Bouchard. Taller than most of his peers and sturdily built, Bouchard was better suited for artillery work below deck than climbing the rigging and furling the sails of the 55-meter warship.

Le Genereux seemed charmed. Originally launched in 1785, she had been spared in the fires of Toulon harbor and escaped the destruction of the French fleet at Aboukir, Egypt. The following year she participated in the successful bombardment of Brindisi and claimed a victory over the 50-gun British frigate *Leander,* capturing its crew, including Nelson's flag captain, Sir Edward Berry. It would not *be le Genereux's* last encounter with Captain Berry.

Although otherwise distracted by his passionate and public affair with Emma, Lady Hamilton, wife of the British ambassador on Sicily, Lord Nelson ordered the British fleet to increase the pressure of the blockade. While Vice Admiral Lord Keith, aboard *HMS Queen Charlotte,* kept the vigil at the harbor mouth, he ordered ships *Foudroyant, Audacious, and Northumberland* to close in on the approaching French squadron while the *Lion* and *Alexander* gave chase. Meanwhile *HMS Success* had been shadowing the French convoy across the Mediterranean. Surrounded by closing British ships, *le Genereux* prepared for battle. On the lower deck, Bouchard tested his strength loading the 36 pounders into the cannons and straining at the restraining ropes on the gun carriages. After capturing one of the French transports, the *Success* engaged the much larger *le Genereux,* crossing in front of the French ship's bow and firing several broadsides, before the larger ship could turn and return fire. British shrapnel or splinters temporarily blinded *Contre-Admiral* (rear admiral) Jean-Baptiste Perrie. Both ships sustained damage with the first volleys. On her second broadside, a cannon ball from *Success* tore off the French admiral's leg and he fell mortally wounded on the deck of his flagship. He would be the only French casualty of the battle. *HMS Foudroyant*, under Captain Edward Berry and with Nelson aboard, along with *HMS Northumberland,* quickly closed and l*e Genereux,* surrounded and vastly outgunned, struck her colors (the enormous, captured tricolor battle flag would be displayed at Norwich, England and still can be seen there). The surrender was taken by Captain Berry. In the melee, the rest of the French convoy escaped to open waters and sailed back toward the French coast. None of the supplies or reinforcements would ever reach Malta, which held out for several more months before finally capitulating in September 1800.[5.] The Island of Malta remained a British colony until independence in 1974.

Andre-Paul Bouchard found himself prisoner aboard his own ship. Although damaged, *le Genereux* was still seaworthy. Lord Nelson, pleased to have removed yet another French ship that he had faced at Battle of the Nile, ordered the ship to sail to British-held Minorca, in the Balearic Islands off the coast of Spain, for repair, under command of Lieutenant Lord Thomas Cochrane. Twenty years later, Cochrane and Bouchard would again confront each other over the issue of piracy in a different war, in a different ocean. As for *le Genereux,* it would be re-commissioned as *HMS Genereux* in British service before being moored at Portsmouth between *Temeraine,* Horatio Nelson's second ship at Trafalgar, and *Vanguard,* his flagship at the Nile. *Le/HMS Genereux* was scrapped in 1816.

With the onset of war with France, England needed a safe harbor in the Mediterranean. Malta was contested by the French, so British strategy revolved around a secure base at Port Mahon, on the Balearic Island of Minorca (also spelled Menorca). In November 1798, a British convoy under Lord St. Vincent had transported troops commanded by General Charles Stuart, who landed at Addaya and chased the local Spaniards back to Port Mahon without a fight.

> *"The possession of Port Mahon in a war with France and Spain combined, provided a base for the fleet whence the Spanish coast could be harassed and the approaches to Toulon watched and hindered"* [6]

Interestingly, General Stuart had licensed twelve Minorcan vessels as privateers with letters of marque by early 1799.

Minorca proved to be a pleasant interlude. The climate was agreeable, and the French prisoners were apparently well treated. The island offered a wide variety of fresh food and many of the islanders looked more favorably toward the French than the British. Under British administration, the Minorcans enjoyed a spurt of prosperity. After a brief confinement, the French prisoners were paroled. Minorca continued to be an important British naval base until it was ceded back to Spain with the Peace of Amiens in 1802 (the Balearic Islands remain an autonomous province of Spain today), by which Britain ended hostilities with France and recognized the French Republic. The peace lasted only a year. However, after Nelson's decisive victory at Trafalgar (1805) even without Minorca, but with Gibraltar at one end and Malta at the other, the Mediterranean would become a British pond for more than a century.

Repatriated to France, battle-tested Andre-Paul made a quick visit to his family in Saint Tropez but found his new stepfather intolerable. He made his way back to Toulon and prepared for a new naval campaign that would take him far from the familiarity of Europe and the Mediterranean. In December 1801 or January 1802, Bouchard sailed with an armada of some 50 ships to the Caribbean colony of Saint-Domingue. The experience would relocate the young sailor to the Americas and predetermine the arc of his brilliant career.

Saint-Domingue – later called Haiti – occupied the western half of the island of Hispaniola. It was France's cash cow. Its sugar plantations made it the wealthiest colony in the world. It supplied half of Europe's tropical produce. Maintaining this economic windfall required massive amounts of human capital in the form of enslaved Africans – as many as a third of the total global trans-Atlantic slave trade. Managing this slave work force, which represented nine of ten inhabitants on the island, was accomplished with extreme cruelty, sadistic punishments and unspeakable violence. Inspired, in part by the ideals of the French Revolution, the slaves of Saint-Domingue had rebelled in 1791 and accomplished the first successful slave revolution of the modern world, establishing an independent nation by 1804. Matching the French level of violence, the slaves had murdered their overseers, burned the cane fields and plantations and driven the French out of Saint-Domingue. The ruling class of plantation owners and French investors would not allow this situation to continue.

To regain control, French authorities granted freedom and French citizenship to former enslaved peoples. In 1794 the French revolutionary government had abolished slavery in all French colonies. (It would be decades before Britain outlawed slavery and half a century before the American Civil War accomplished the same thing). However, in a cynical turnabout, First Consul Napoleon reinstated the slave trade. In 1801, in a move to remove the former slave-turned-leader of the independent Haiti, Toussaint L'Ouverture, and reassert French control, Napoleon ordered a massive military campaign against the Caribbean Island[7] It did not go well.

Historian Gordon Wright concludes,

> *"Bonaparte's only serious failure during the early years was the frustration of his colonial plans [which included expansion in the Caribbean and Louisiana]. His ambitions ranged to every continent but only in America did he embark on a practical program. His attempt to reconquer (sic) the rich sugar island of Haiti ended in disaster; guerilla warfare and fever decimated his troops. The renewal of war with England made communications impossible; Bonaparte withdrew the remains of his expeditionary force and cut his loses by selling Louisiana territory."*[8]

Napoleon would lose more troops in Haiti than at Waterloo.

More than two thirds of the French navy was allocated to the campaign against Saint-Domingue. Tens of thousands of soldiers and sailors mustered at Brest, Cadiz, Toulon and other ports and crowded on dozens of ships of the line, frigates and transports. Logistical problems plagued the fleet from the onset. Toulon had expected 500 troops and received some 3,000. Many of the ships were stripped of their guns to accommodate even more troops but rendering them defenseless. Bouchard was assigned to the crew of the frigate *Badine,* one of the Malta convoy ships that had escaped capture. Without armament, artillerymen such as Bouchard were reduced to supplementary sea duties, the first of many frustrations. Soldiers and sailors slept on the overcrowded decks in the open during the month-long passage across the Atlantic following the route originally sailed by Columbus in his voyages of discovery three centuries earlier.

The historical record lacks specifics about the service of individual sailors in the Saint Domingue campaign. But sufficient naval and other records describe the role of the French navy in sufficient detail to reconstruct what seaman Bouchard experienced. From the beginning the navy was relegated to a subordinate role to the army, which clearly was Napoleon's focus. The First Consul's grasp of naval affairs showed none of his genius for land strategy. Military leaders, aware of the navy's poor prior record compared with the army's, proved it to be a self-fulfilling prophecy and they failed to allow the navy to operate effectively. In many instances, the navy was reduced to ferrying troops and evacuation efforts. The expedition proved costly to the navy, losing ten ships of the line and scores of smaller vessels. Over 8,000 sailors, a tenth of the entire French navy, died, many from yellow fever. The tropical climate quickly reduced the condition of many of the ships. And there was the revolting routine practice of taking prisoners of war, almost all black former slaves, and drowning them at sea. With low expectations and even lower duties, the French navy was quickly demoralized and in turn contributed to the French defeat. [9]

In less than two years, the Haitians had destroyed much of Napoleon's forces and destroyed his dreams of empire in America. He would next turn his attention east toward Russia. Though the Haitians declared independence in 1804, no other nation would recognize the new nation, unwilling to encourage a slave revolt in their own countries. Haiti knew the French would not give up so easily. Return they did. In 1825, under the auspices of the restored Bourbon King Charles X, a French envoy sailed into the capital at Port-au-Prince with an offer to recognize Haitian independence in return for preferential taxation on imported French goods and reparations of a staggering 150 million French francs. It was blatant extortion, backed by a threat of overwhelming French military force. Under the gun, Haiti accepted the terms everyone knew they could not meet. Forced to borrow from French banks to repay the French reparations, Haiti was consigned to perpetual debt in what was described as "perhaps the single most odious sovereign debt in history." As a result, the proud nation of former slaves remained among the poorest of nations in perpetuity. [10]

Throughout the revolutionary and Napoleonic periods, the French navy had been a constant threat to its enemies, although its potential danger exceeded its actual performance. While the principle of e*galite* heralded new opportunities for the masses, it destroyed the naval command structure. Aristocratic officers, who had nevertheless performed so well during the North American revolution, were cashiered from service, replaced by inexperienced men. Crews were often supplemented with prisoners. The navy became an unattractive occupation for many, especially compared to the *Grand Armee.* It was chronically underfunded by the government and its supply of ships never met the demand. In time, a defeatist mentality crept in from the admirals to the newest recruits. In the end, the navy failed both the revolution and the emperor.[11]

In a humiliating denouement to the Napoleonic misadventure in Haiti, the ragged balance of his forces was stopped by the British blockade while trying to evacuate in November 1802. Many French prisoners were sent to pontoon prison boats in Jamaica. Other survivors found refuge in Spanish held Santo Domingo (the eastern half of Hispaniola), Cuba, or French colonies on Martinique and Guadeloupe.[12] Unhappy with the French drift away from the liberal policies of the Revolution, sometime before the Haitian collapse, Andre-Paul Bouchard distanced himself emotionally and then physically from the Haitian debacle. History fails to provide an accounting of the next few years. He likely may have returned to France with his ship and mustered out of the Navy, only to return to the Americas. Alternately, he may simply have deserted and remained in the Caribbean. At this time, he seems to have abandoned his given names in exchange for using his youngest brother's first name, Hippolyte. (It is unclear whether this was an effort to confuse his identity or possibly a homage to his younger sibling, whom he may have felt he had abandoned. (A more prosaic explanation may be that as Bouchard entered a Spanish-speaking world, the diminutive form of Paul in Spanish, *Polito,* may have been further bastardized into *Hipolito*, with a variety of spellings. He would later sign correspondence *Hipaulito).* In any event, Bouchard likely found himself in Santiago, Cuba, which had become a center of smuggling, trade and privateering in the Caribbean or on one of the remaining French island possessions such as Guadalupe or Martinique. While Bouchard probably did not begin his privateering career there by directly attacking his own native country's ships, he quite possibly engaged in some seafaring that bordered on illegal. And feeling that France – Napoleon in particular – had betrayed the ideals of the Revolution, he sought new masters and new causes to serve.

Like many, Hipolito Bouchard was drawn to the United States, where the opportunities appeared greater than under any European flag, and the idealism of the American revolution seemed intact. The United States had an expanding naval and merchant marine presence. Baltimore, Maryland had become a major shipbuilding center and port-of-call for cargo and passengers. There in the deep-water port on the northwest shore of the Chesapeake Bay, skilled craftsmen built the unique Baltimore Clippers, smaller sized sailing schooners, notoriously used by coastal raiders and privateers. Ships from many nations docked there and agents from many parts of the Americas were customers of the shipyards. Crews with experience were constantly in demand and he would have been able to hone his navigational skills. Bouchard would crew vessels sailing under many flags over the coming years, though there is no evidence that he sailed under the black flag of piracy, which by that time had been largely swept from the seas. His voyages took him from the Atlantic seaboard of North America, through the hurricane-plagued islands of the Caribbean, to mainland ports at Vera Cruz, Panama, Cartagena, Rio de Janeiro and Buenos Aires, as well as any number of nameless smugglers' inlets and bays. As his world expanded, his skill as a seaman grew to match his ambition. He moved quickly from below deck to mid-ship. He lived the life of an international wanderer. Many of his shipmates had chosen the sea to escape their previous lives. They spoke English, French, Spanish, Portuguese or Dutch and he learned smatterings of them all.

In the harbor taverns up and down the Atlantic coast stories of foreign trade, intrigue, romance and wars were told and retold over tankard tops, including tales of the efforts in Mexico and South America to throw off the long rule of Spain. Spain still controlled most of the western hemisphere south and west of the United States and Spanish ports officially restricted trade to only their own shipping. Unofficially, foreign traders and smugglers found ready markets for contraband in Central and South America. Bouchard held no love for imperial Spain or its monarchy. He had been imprisoned on Minorca and may have traveled through Spain after his release, enroute back to France. And Spain represented everything the *Rights of Man and the Citizen* opposed. Perhaps in Argentina, his revolutionary ideals could make a difference.

Notes:

1. Stanley Hoffmann, In Search of France, New York: Harper & Row, 1963, p. 1.
2. John C. Cairns, France, Englewood Cliffs: New Jersey, Spectrum Books, 1965, p. 27.
3. Ibid.
4. Gordon Wright, France in Modern Times, Chicago: Rand McNally & Co., 1966, p. 88.
5. "Maltese History & Heritage," https://www.vassallohistory.wordpress.com>frenchblockade. Retrieved July 5, 2022.
6. Sir Clements R. Markham, The Story of Majorca and Minorca, London: Smith, Elder & Co., 1908, p. 285.
7. Catherine Porter, Constant Meheut, Matt Apuzzo and Selam Gebrekidan, "A land of Riches, but Not for its Own People," *New York Times,* May 22, 2022.
8. Gordon Wright, op. cit., p. 90.
9. Philippe R. Girard, "The Ugly Duckling: The French Navy and the Saint-Domingue Expedition, 1801-1803," *International Journal of Naval History,* December 1, 2010.
10. Catherine Porter et al., op.cit.
11. Dominic Annen, "Triocolor and Union Jack at Sea: How the French Revolution Decapitated Napoleon's Navy and Thereby Ruined His Ambitions," (2015) Student Theses, Papers and Projects (History), 43, https://digitalcommons.wou.edu/his/43.
12. Philippe R. Gerard, op. cit.

Chapter 3
The Call of Liberty

"The Voice of the people is the will of God."

–Argentine Proverb

"Solo quiero Leones en mi regimiento." ("I only want lions in my regiment.")

–Jose de San Martin, quoted in *San Martin, The Liberator* (1971), by J.C.J. Metford

Buenos Aires, 1810. After a year since his arrival, Hipolito Bouchard had grown accustomed to his new home in Buenos Aires. He still made his living as a seaman, occasionally crewing a schooner taking salted beef, leather and tallow to the Portuguese colony of Brazil, but more often ferrying goods and passengers farther up the Rio de la Plata estuary and Parana River or across to Montevideo. With work constantly available in the dockyards and on the many ships using the port of Buenos Aires, he earned enough to afford shared lodging nearby on the periphery of the grid-patterned city. He stayed strong on the local protein-rich diet of beef, bread and *mate,* a sort of tea brewed from the leaves of the *yerba mate* plant. Increasingly he felt more at home in this South American boomtown so far from everywhere else. There was an energy here; a sense of political uncertainty that had everyone on alert.

The Spaniards had claimed dominion over most of the New World as result of the papal Treaty of Tordesillas (1494) and backed up their claim by conquering the vast empires of the Aztecs in modern Mexico and the Incas in South America in the 16th century. For three hundred years, the mineral wealth – principally silver, thus the name for both the river *Plata* and the country *Argentina* – was mined from the bones of the American continents by forced labor and sent back to fill the coffers of Spain in enormous quantities. In 1515 the Spanish commander Juan Diaz de Solis sailed south to the mouth of the Rio de la Plata (River of Silver). On the muddy marshland along of the river, a settlement was initially founded as Nuestra Senora Santa Maria del Buen Ayre (Our Lady Holy Mary of Good Air) by an expedition led by Pedro de Mendoza in 1536. However, the settlement was largely abandoned for several decades in favor of other locations further inland and to the north. The city was later reoccupied by the beginning of the 1600s to block Portuguese expansion from Brazil.

Beyond the periphery of the city stretched the vast fertile *pampas* grasslands, where the descendants of horses and cattle originally brought by the Mendoza expedition had multiplied to establish the base of a great cattle empire, formed around large *estancias* (ranches).

Seeking autonomy, Jesuit missionaries had established their own settlements west toward the foothills of the towering Andes Mountains. Indigenous peoples were brought to the Christian religion and made to provide the local labor force, later supplemented by large numbers of imported Africans as slaves. The Argentine colony was administered from Lima, Peru until the 18th century, when this arrangement proved too unwieldy. With an expanding population and economy, the Viceroyalty of Rio de la Plata was split off from the Viceroyalty of Peru in 1776. Buenos Aires was now free of many of the restrictions previously imposed by Lima. It was becoming an important international port. And despite Madrid's efforts to censor foreign news, arriving ships from Europe and American cities brought details of the French and North American Revolutions, Napoleon's conquests, as well as of the slave rebellion and independence in Haiti. The Enlightenment ideas of the new world order were finding their way throughout the "New World."

At the turn of the 19th century, a ship sailing between the Spanish mother country and Buenos Aires still took as long as several months, depending upon weather or interference by enemy ships or privateers. Even the cruise from the Caribbean took several weeks. But despite the time and distance separating South America from the Spanish homeland and the rest of the world, Argentina did not exist in isolation. Events internally in the Rio de la Plata capital were developing a momentum of their own, but those events were very much initiated by events abroad, particularly in Europe.

In 1805, the British achieved a spectacular naval victory destroying both the French fleet and allied Spanish fleet at Trafalgar, while suffering little loss themselves (although aboard the ironically named *HMS Victory*, a French sharpshooter's bullet took the life of Admiral Horatio Nelson). Without naval support, Napoleon was forced to scuttle plans for an invasion of Britain, instead focusing on consolidating his continental empire. As Napoleonic Wars scholar Jeremy Black writes,

> *"Naval strength and colonial power were the basis of Britain's ability to sustain its own war effort and to provide support to allies."* [1]

Supreme at sea, the British fleet was free to attend to its colonies around the globe and probe the weaknesses of its enemies. In 1807 a small British expeditionary force sailed into the Rio de la Plata estuary and occupied Buenos Aires for several weeks before being repulsed by local militia under the leadership of French-born former Spanish naval officer named Santiago de Liniers y Bremond. "Despite his French nationality he was a highly visible member of the regional elite in 1806, his status due to noble birth and to the wealth and social connections of his father-in-law."[2] Anticipating the British return, Liniers and others recruited and trained a civilian militia. A year later a larger British force reappeared in the estuary and encountered heavy armed resistance in the narrow streets of Buenos Aires. After suffering heavy losses, British Lieutenant-General John Whitelocke abandoned the effort and returned to England in disgrace. Santiago de Liniers was popularly elected provisional viceroy in lieu of anyone sent from Madrid's "illegitimate" government in exile. These events convinced the *portenos* ("people of the port", as the citizens of Buenos Aires were known) that they could no longer count on protection and defense by Spanish forces. Perhaps more significantly, by withstanding a foreign power, they began to sense the possibility of self-determination. After the gun smoke blew away a faint whiff of independence remained.

On the Iberian Peninsula, Napoleon had achieved a quick occupation of Portugal, as punishment for Lisbon's alliance with Britain. Next, he turned his attention to former ally Spain. He overran the country, forced King Ferdinand VII into abdication, and installed his own brother, Joseph, as king. These events ignited the protracted, guerilla Peninsular War. With their king deposed, the Spanish people in rebellion against the French and the Spanish government effectively neutered, the loyal people of Argentina began to look to themselves for leadership.

At the top of the Argentine social pyramid sat the *peninsulares,* Spanish nobles and aristocrats of European birth, *llegadas (*arrivals*)* from their native Spain, occupying positions of power and privilege, with no intention of ceding any of it away. They were counterpointed by the larger class of *criollos* (creoles), ethnic Spaniards born in the Americas. This class had grown significantly over the generations and increasingly resented the restrictions placed upon them by the *peninsulares* and Madrid. Many *criollos* were, in fact, European educated and had served in the Spanish military. They considered themselves equal to the *peninsulares* in every way, and as native-born Americans, they perhaps had an even greater claim to running local affairs. Below the power elite were the middle-class artisans, merchants, immigrants such as Bouchard, and foreign born or ethnic landowners in a bewildering hierarchy known as *castas*. Supporting all of these were the people of mixed race, indigenous descent or African slaves who made up the working class and the dispossessed.

So it was that in May 1810, Hipolito Bouchard was drawn to the crowd gathering in the Plaza Mayor outside the Cabildo (city hall), where a *cabildo abierto* (open public forum) had been called to discuss the future of the viceroyalty of Rio de la Plata. The Spanish government had been reduced to a fragile junta in Cadiz. Fissures in the Spanish control of the four American viceroyalties of New Spain, New Granada, Peru and Rio de la Plata were widening daily. Bouchard noted the presence of soldiers in the main square and that many in the crowd were also armed. The week ended with the replacement of the Spanish-appointed viceroy and the orchestrated establishment of a junta government controlled by nationalists rather than Spanish loyalists. The movement toward independence had begun. A child of revolutionary France and an avowed anti-monarchist, Bouchard was caught up in the moment and longed to play a part. Soon he would.

Latin American historian John Lynch, in his book *San Martin. Argentine Soldier. American Hero* characterized the May 10 Revolution as,

> *"more than an extension of the resistance and junta movement in Spain, more than a bid for self-government under the Crown. It was the revolt of a colony, led by radical and violent revolutionaries, whose loyalty to a captive king cannot be taken seriously."*[3]

The breakaway region would be known as The United Provinces of Rio de la Plata. (It would not be called Argentina until many years after national independence. This narrative will use both the terms *Argentina* and *Argentine and United Provinces de la Plata generically* to avoid confusion.)

Though weakened, the Spanish royalists were not yet impotent and regrouped at Montevideo, on the opposite bank of the de la Plata estuary. They regarded anything less than total allegiance to their abdicated king to be seditious treason. To prevent the Spanish from navigating farther upriver and securing territory inland, the revolutionaries cobbled together a flotilla of mismatched ships to blockade upriver from Montevideo. With the royalists still in control of whatever Spanish navy personnel were in the area, the insurgents recruited experienced sailors from the general public. Sympathetic to the cause and seizing the opportunity to distinguish himself, Bouchard offered his services. While lacking captain's papers, he certainly made up for it in experience and was granted captaincy of *the 25 de Mayo,* his first command. Off the Parana riverbank near the village of San Nicolas de los Arroyos, the revolutionaries encountered a Spanish squadron. Outnumbered, out-gunned and out-sailed, the rebels' ships were quickly disabled. Bouchard's crew, an assortment of sailors and landlubbers, many of whom literally had no political oar in this fight, panicked and began abandoning ship.

Furious at his loss of control and unable to stop the flight, Bouchard ultimately jumped from the ship himself and swam to shore to avoid capture. In Buenos Aires, Bouchard and the others were put on trial for the loss of the ships. The tribunal acknowledged Bouchard's bravery and attempts to retain discipline during the engagement, and he was exonerated. But a faint odor of cowardice would follow him for many years, nevertheless.

Months later, the Spanish royalists decided to make an object lesson of Buenos Aires by initiating an offshore bombardment. The besieged city stiffened its resolve. A hastily reconstituted fleet checked the advance of a subsequent Spanish attack and Bouchard, now captain of the *Santo Domingo,* was singled out for his bravery – a partial redemption for the San Nicolas debacle. Once again, the revolutionaries disbanded the fledgling navy and Bouchard was left a captain without a ship. But he was becoming known in the political and social circles of Buenos Aires.

Navigating the hierarchical social system of colonial Buenos Aires challenged Bouchard. He was neither a *peninsular* nor *criollo* Spaniard, but an immigrant Frenchman. His ethnicity made him suspect as a closet Bonapartist or radical revolutionary. His heavily accented Spanish brought stares of scorn or even humor. His manners were often as course as his rough seaman's hands and his disposition ranged from brusque to obnoxious. Nevertheless, he was a presence to be reckoned with. In the first instance, he was physically imposing, tall, broad shouldered, with dark features and darker hair. His service in the defense of Buenos Aires provided a certain entre to society and his strong republican views found favor among like-minded members of the evolving middle class who made introductions for him. Upward mobility in Buenos Aires often centered around family connections. He became associated with the well-connected family of merchant Gregorio Ramon de Merlo y Gamiz and became engaged to his daughter, Norberta. They were married by the chaplain in a military ceremony on April 8, 1812.

Maria Noventa Josefa de Corazon de Jesus Merlo Diaz, commonly known as Norberta, was born June 5, 1794, and baptized two years later at Parroquia de Nuestra Senora de la Merced in Buenos Aires. Her mother was Lugarda Francisca Diaz Fravega, the third wife of Gregorio de Merlo. Her grandfather, Francisco Javiaer de Merlo y Barboza had been born in Seville, Spain in 1693 and sent to South America. Francisco de Merlo was appointed a public notary by the Spanish Crown and in 1726 he had participated in the founding of the city of Montevideo. In 1734 he became notary of the Cabildo of Buenos Aires. De Merlo acquired extensive land holdings and created the town of San Antonio del Camino, west of Buenos Aires. The Merlo region expanded over the decades until it was incorporated into the greater Buenos Aires metropolitan area in the early 20th century. Merlo descendants are still prominent in Buenos Aires today. With these family connections, Hipolito Bouchard had leverage to assert himself and pursue his ambitions. Together, he and Norberta would begin a family; their first child Maria del Carmen, was born in 1813. However, his life away at sea would take him from his family. He never held his youngest daughter, Fermina, born in July 1817, weeks after he sailed away for good.

The war for independence faced multiple opponents: Imperial Spain, otherwise occupied fighting against Napoleon; the domestic royalists who maintained allegiance to the deposed king and the temporary junta in Cadiz, Spain, trying to rule what was still free of the French; and the provinces surrounding Buenos Aires, such as Banda Oriental (modern Uruguay), Paraguay and Upper Peru (modern Bolivia), which may have favored independence but also preferred autonomy from Buenos Aires. Military leadership was coalescing around a young *criollo* soldier recently returned from living in Spain and a veteran officer of the Spanish army in the Peninsular War, Jose de San Martin.

Jose Francisco de San Martin y Matorras was born Feb. 2, 1778, at Yapeyu, along the Upper Uruguay River. His birth mother may have been an indigenous Guarani woman. His adoptive father, Juan Jose de San Martin y Gomez, was a native of Palencia, Spain who had been sent to Argentina as the first lieutenant governor of the Guarani missions at Yapeyu, previously run by the Jesuit Order before their expulsion from the country. The San Martin family returned to Spain in 1783, where young Jose was educated in Madrid and began a military career at age eleven. He rose steadily through the ranks and acquitted himself well in several campaigns. During the Peninsular War he received the Heroes' Gold Medal at the Battle of Bellen, which allowed the Spaniards to retake Madrid. While serving with British allies, San Martin became introduced to and initiated into secret lodges, associated with freemasonry, conspiring toward South American independence. In 1811, San Martin resigned his Spanish commission and, after a brief stay in London where he engaged with several prominent independence movement leaders, or *independistas,* returned to his homeland, offering his services to the United Provinces of the Rio de la Plata. Believing independence from Spain would require unity among all parts of South America, Jose de San Martin would go on to liberate three future nations: Argentina, Chile and Peru. He is considered by many the co-equal of that other great South American *Libertador*, Simon Bolivar.

Despite some suspicion over his switch of allegiance from the Spanish Crown to the rebel cause, the ruling triumvirate quickly offered San Martin the command of a new cavalry unit. San Martin recognized that the United Provinces would need more than an armed militia to stand against trained European professional soldiers. San Martin set about recruiting for an elite squadron called the *Granaderos de Caballo* (Grenadier Cavalry), modeled after the modern tactics from the European theatre of war. Increasingly, military service was being used to advance in local society. With no sign of the government restoring the navy, Hipolito Bouchard volunteered for the *Granaderos*, training with much younger recruits. Many of the recruits were also former *gauchos,* the skilled horsemen of the *pampas*. Bouchard would compensate for any deficiencies in equestrian skills by single minded determination – and extreme bravery in the battle to come. In February 1818, San Martin led his unit to the port of San Lorenzo to block royalist incursion up the Parana River. Heavily outnumbered, the *Granaderos* engaged a Spanish landing force in front of the Convent of San Carlos. Despite covering fire from the Spanish ships, San Martin led a surprise cavalry charge from the front until his horse was shot out from under him. An enraged Hipolito Bouchard charged the Spanish standard bearer, killing him with a sword thrust and capturing the enemy flag. In his governmental report of the battle, San Martin singled out *"the brave officer Don Hipolito Bouchard"* by name. The stain of San Nicolas was further erased; it would not be the last time Bouchard would seek redemption.

San Martin rewarded the tall Frenchman with promotion *to capitan de los granaderos,* but his victory at San Lorenzo was criticized for having let the Spanish forces escape back to their ships. San Martin was temporarily reassigned a defensive role at Buenos Aires. Bouchard found such garrison duties frustrating. At the end of 1813, San Martin was called to reinforce General Manuel Belgrano's beleaguered forces in the north of the province. Bouchard became disgruntled at the long march into the unforgiving landscape of the continental interior, without any sign of the enemy. His disaffection intensified with an illness that lasted weeks. When news arrived that the navy was being reformed, Bouchard lobbied hard to be reassigned. San Martin resented this junior officer requesting the transfer, but eventually approved it, hoping to rid his unit of a morale-sapping complainer. As Hipolito Bouchard made his way back toward the coast, Jose de San Martin was now free to exert his leadership in the war.

As biographer John Lynch described it,

> *"He had come to Buenos Aires to serve a wider cause than the provincial policies of the Rio de la Plata, convinced military power should serve an American purpose and not a mere local interest...he now had the chance to fulfil his greater mission, to define the revolution anew, to expand horizons from country to continent and to establish a new base for the war of independence."* [4]

Hipolito Bouchard would not accompany Jose de San Martin on campaigns in Upper Peru or his heroic crossing of the Andes to liberate Chile. Instead, Bouchard would play his own role in the war for independence, back on the rolling deck of a ship. He was going back to the sea.

Notes:

1. Jeremy Black, The French Revolutionary and Napoleonic Wars. Strategies for a World War, Lanham, MD: Rowman & Littlefield, 2022, p. 64.
2. Lyman L. Johnson, Workshop of Revolution. Plebeian Buenos Aires and the Atlantic World, 1776-1810, Durham, NC: Duke University Press, 2011, pp. 252-253.
3. John Lynch, San Martin. Argentine Soldier. American Hero, New Haven, CT: Yale University Press, 2009, p. 38.
4. Ibid, p. 54.

Chapter 4
Drake's Ghost

"Familiarity with danger makes a brave man braver, but less daring. This with seamen, he who goes the offenest round Cape Horn goes the most circumspectly."

–Herman Melville, *White Jacket*, 1850

"It isn't that life ashore is distasteful to me. But life at sea is better."

–Sir Francis Drake (c. 1540-96)

"The natural history of this archipelago is very remarkable; it seems to be a little world within itself."

–Charles Darwin, *Voyage of the Beagle*, 1839,
Reflecting upon the Galapagos Islands

With the onset of the French Revolution, many of the aristocratic French naval officers had been purged. Several had fled France, taking valuable command experience gained during the American War for Independence with them. At the end of the Napoleonic Wars, several belligerent nations demilitarized, downsizing their navies and throwing thousands of naval officers and seamen into unemployment. Many of the officer class sought positions with the fleets of other nations. The concern was less a question of national security or loyalty, but rather of competition in a flooded job market. "Several types of foreign-born men could be found on naval quarterdecks and in naval wardrooms…career prospects were ultimately dictated by the state of the employment market."[1]

At the end of the second American War with Great Britain, 1812-14, thousands of seamen were also made redundant as the American Navy once again constricted. Some found work as fishermen, particularly off the Grand Banks of the North Atlantic. Many others became merchant seamen sailing for dozens of different nations. Thousands more found opportunities as privateers, sailing in substitution of their own country's regular navy, or more likely under the flags of other nations and the insurgent governments during the Spanish American wars of independence. As Hipolito Bouchard had learned, place of origin was superseded by the demands for experienced mariners with battle experience. As the new United Provinces de Rio de la Plata recognized that it must also confront Spain on the seas, it would be an Irish immigrant merchant sea captain named William Brown who would resurrect and make permanent the Argentine navy, becoming, along with Jose de San Martin, a father of his country.

William Brown came from lowly birth in Foxford, County Mayo, Ireland in 1777, but as a boy seemingly had found a sponsor in Admiral Lord Howe of the British Navy, who secured him a position as a midshipman in the Royal Navy. Brown switched from the navy to the merchant fleet and was captured by the French corvette *Presidente* in 1801. Upon release, he resumed his career with the merchant fleet, sailing in the West Indies. In 1809 he married Eliza Chitty, daughter in a prominent Kentish family of Channel pilots, seamen and privateers. That same year he made his first visit to Rio de la Plata. He became a partner in the *Eliza,* a captured French privateer, formerly *the Grand Napoleon, and* soon mastered the shifting sand banks of the Rio de la Plata and the seasonal *pamperos,* the unpredictable winds off the *pampas,* shipping cargo from the Argentine side of the river to the Uruguayan bank on the other.

With the independence movement, Brown became a serious blockade runner, avoiding the Spanish patrols aimed at stopping his mercantile efforts. When the Spanish effectively blockaded Buenos Aires from both the mouth of the estuary and the confluence of the Parana and Uruguay Rivers upstream, Brown reluctantly accepted commission as a lieutenant colonel and commander-in-chief of the new navy. In 1814, aboard a former Russian merchant ship, renamed *Hercules,* and accompanied by ships *Tortugas, Fortunata* and a felucca (a small, open boat with a large triangular sail, common to the Nile River in Egypt) sailed the twenty miles to the fortified island of Martin Garcia, which guarded access to the two rivers. After a furious land and sea assault, lasting several days, the island fell to the insurgents. Brown next chased the Spanish fleet back to Montevideo, which now found itself cut off by Brown's fleet. After weeks of blockade, Brown lured the Spanish fleet away from the protective guns of Montevideo, surprised the enemy and destroyed or captured their ships. The Spanish grip on Rio de la Plata was broken for good as Montevideo fell to the rebels. Gravely wounded in the leg by a cannon ball, Brown nevertheless was proclaimed a national hero by the *portenos* of Buenos Aires. His career was only just beginning. [2]

By the time Hipolito Bouchard and his company of *granaderos* arrived back in Buenos Aires from Upper Peru, things were quiet. The Spanish had been driven from both ends of the river and the royalist stronghold of Montevideo was no longer held by those appointed by Madrid. Any talk of the navy in the local *pulperias* (local bars serving fermented juice) revolved around the heroic exploits of William (known colloquially as Guillermo) Brown.

Bouchard's reputation as a troublemaker had proceeded him. He found himself reduced in rank from his captaincy in the *granaderos* and unable to find a suitable command in the once-again idle navy. Instead, he was given a bureaucratic clerk's job in the port of Buenos Aires. Compounding his problems was disclosure of his personal correspondence criticizing certain local government officials, including a close Merlo family friend who had even stood with Bouchard at his wedding. Yet he continued his outspoken ways. His political sentiments were called into question. Militarily, socially and politically he was becoming a pariah. And he was bringing shame to his family, now including his first-born daughter, Carmen, born in 1813. Bouchard found himself in a dark place of his own creation.

While Bouchard's career languished, the provisional government of the United Provinces began to resemble the chaotic Directorate of Revolutionary France. In the sudden shifting of political fortunes, Supreme Director Gervasio Antonio Posadas, the close Merlo family associate, was overthrown. In succession, he was replaced by his own nephew Carlos Maria de Alvear. Alvear, who had accompanied San Martin as a friend on his return to Argentina from Europe and would become San Martin's political rival, was subsequently overthrown, himself, in a *coup d'état*. Bouchard had openly been critical of Alvear as well, despite the fact he had been a witness at Bouchard's wedding. Now many of Bouchard's outbursts seemed more politically correct. Like a sailor who knows when to set sail to catch a new wind, Bouchard reached out to the one person who seemed to be above the fray, *Almirante* (Admiral) Guillermo Brown.

As much by coincidence as by cooperation, both San Martin and William Brown had settled on the same grand strategy: in order to dislodge the Spanish, the fight would have to shift from the east side of the Andes to the Pacific side on the west. For San Martin, that would entail taking his army over the Andes cordillera, the longest mountain chain in the world, recalling Hannibal's epic crossing of the Alps. For Admiral Brown, it meant sailing around Cape Horn and attacking Spanish shipping and ports in Chile and Peru itself. Despite the victories at Martin Garcia and Montevideo, all previous efforts to sustain an Argentine navy had faltered. The alternative solution appeared to be institutionalizing the age-old use of privateers. It would fall to Brown to organize a sea force of *corsarios.* And for Bouchard, it seemed his last, best chance.

Luckily, Bouchard still had a couple of important allies, including Juan Martin de Pueyrredon, the new head of state, and Vicente Anastasio de Echevarria, a wealthy and influential *porteno* lawyer who had been deeply involved in the revolutionary movement from the beginning. With this backing, Bouchard was able to convince Admiral Brown to include him in the new privateer expedition being planned. Privateering was a game played by nations with very specific rules. Under ordinary circumstances what would be considered piracy was considered legitimate as long as everybody accepted the rules. And of course, privateers sometimes adjusted the rules as the situations called for, or simply rewrote the rules. The greatest advantage to the state was that privateers could seriously interrupt enemy commerce and inflict considerable damage with minimal cost to the state which would also take a cut of any booty captured. Besides patriotism, wealthy investors were motivated to willingly accept the risk to buy and outfit a privateering ship, betting on the possibility of reaping as much as half of any prizes seized as spoils of war. Captaining a privateer cloaked many a would-be pirate in a veneer of patriot sailor and a captured enemy treasure ship could mean a comfortable retirement. It was agreed that the state would receive a one-ninth share of any plunder; Brown would receive two-ninths, and the rest would be divided among the others according to rank. During the independence wars, an estimated 150 speedy sloops and schooners from the United States alone were purchased as privateers by private Argentine investors granted a letter of marque, a lethal hunting license, from the United Provinces government.

On September 12, 1815, Hipolito Bouchard assumed command of the small, three masted, French-built corvette, *Halcon (Hawk or Falcon),* armed with only a single row of cannon, but also with the more powerful official *corsario* letter of marque. The officer compliment included Englishman Robert Jones, Ramon Freire (future president of Chile) and several other French-born officers. The crew was the usual amalgam of many nationalities and an armed dispute occurred over a challenge to Bouchard's authority, while still in port. The captain's ill-temper prevailed but bad blood remained with the crew for the entire voyage. The small armada included Admiral William Brown and his brother-in-law Captain Walter Chitty commanding the frigate *Hercules*, heavily repaired after the damage sustained at Martin Garcia; his brother Michael (Miguel) Brown commanding *Santisima Trinidad,* and the swift, two masted schooner *Constitucion,* under command of Oliverio Russell, a Scot, its crew primarily Chilean immigrants. In all, the expedition carried 150 guns and 500 sailors. The four ships set sail from Montevideo by the end of October to rendezvous at Mocha Island, a small island mid-way up the coast of Chile in a completely different ocean.

The *Halcon* passed through the muddy effluent at the mouth of the River Plata into the clear South Atlantic and enjoyed calm seas and fair winds as it sailed south along the thousand miles of Patagonian coastline. The warm currents from Brazil and the colder currents up from Antarctica created one of the world's most temperate seas. The crew watched the cormorants and penguins dive for anchovies, while dolphins, porpoise and whales cut through the waves and seals, sea lions and elephant seals migrated off the starboard bow. Conditions steadily worsened as the *Halcon* passed between the Falkland Islands and the mainland and made entry into the Tierra del Fuego (land of fires/smokes) archipelago, where Magellan had first noticed the Indian fires ashore, and headed for the Straits of Magellan and the perilous Drake's Passage.

The choppy seas turned into looming mountains as the waters of two different oceans collided. Though high summer, there was no good season to sail around the Cape. Warm Pacific cyclones and Antarctic sea ice were constant threats. In multiple storms and heavy fog, the *Halcon* lost sight of the *Constitucion*, whose heavy guns made her unwieldy. Unable, some would say unwilling, to search for their sister ship, Bouchard pushed on against the heavy eastward current. Fear gripped the crew of *Halcon*. Hailstorms threatened to shred the sails. Massive indigo waves broke across the bow and icy seas tipped the ship at a 45-degree angle, its yard arms dipping into the water. Freezing rain turned the unfurled sails into solid sheets and young seamen had to shin up icy rigging to beat the canvass pliable with their frost-bitten bare hands. The ship's watch strained to see through fog, sleet and snow to avoid the mountainous snow-capped icebergs whose calving sides threated to smash the wooden vessel. The storm entered its second week. There was talk of turning back, as the ship *Elizabeth* had done from Drake's fleet in 1578, before three of Drake's other ships were lost at sea. Some of the crew called for Bouchard to abandon the mission altogether and become a rogue ship – a pirate. Infuriated, Bouchard stared down the mutineers with death threats and stayed the course, finally finding calmer waters in the Pacific Ocean. Three of the four ships arrived at Mocha Island. Neither the *Constitucion* nor its crew were ever seen again.

On Mocha Island, the small Argentine flotilla made necessary repairs and replenished water and food stores. Mocha Island was a known pirate lair and had been the scene of a confrontation between Sir Francis Drake and the indigenous Mapuche natives centuries earlier. Brown's pair of ships had suffered loss of provisions and had been forced to put ashore in in the Strait of Magellan where four sailors deserted. *Almirante* Brown was greatly disturbed by the fate of *the Constitucion.* He had lost a quarter of his fighting force. Nevertheless, he resolved to take the fight directly to the heart of the enemy. Brown would first attempt to free prisoners held on Juan

Fernandez Island. Next, they would attack Lima, capital of the Peruvian Viceroyalty, itself. It was an audacious plan. For more than 250 years, the Spanish had sailed forth from Lima safely and unchallenged, the Pacific Ocean their proprietary domain. After agreeing how to divide any plunder – Brown and the *Hercules* would get 40 percent, the other two ships would each split the rest [3] – the trio greeted the New Year's Day morning of 1816 with full sails set for the Peruvian mainland. They would rendezvous off Callao, the port of Lima. Meanwhile, a United States frigate, *Indus,* sailing from Rio de Janeiro, arrived in Valparaiso, Chile and alerted authorities to the presence of the *corsarios.* In turn, the royal governor of Chile warned the viceroy in Lima of the possible attack.[4]

The following week, the ships rejoined off the islands in front of the harbor of Callao. Callao had been established in 1537 by conquistador Francisco Pizarro soon after he conquered the Inca Empire and made his capital Ciudad de los Reyes, later Lima, ten miles inland. Callao would serve as shipping point for the Incan gold and silver treasure that was sent to Spain, and thereafter nearly all the mineral and other commodities produced by Peru, Bolivia and Argentina would be carried overland, across the Andes Mountains by mules, and shipped from Callao to Panama, then transferred across the isthmus and freighted to Cuba before eventually being shipped on to the Spanish treasury in Madrid. Callao was also a stop on the route of the famed Manila Galleons, the great treasure ships sailing between the Philippines and Acapulco, Mexico. So much concentrated wealth had long attracted attention of Spain's enemies. Callao had been pillaged by Sir Francis Drake almost immediately after its founding. Drake had sailed along the Chilean coast, raided Valparaiso and attacked the defenseless Callao in February 1579, before chasing after and capturing his richest prize, the treasure *ship Nuestra Senora de Concepcion,* on March 1st off the coast of Panama. The shaken inhabitants of Callao, in a clever play on Drake's name, would for generations warn their children about *"El Draque*" (the Dragon).

The *Fuerte* (fort) *del Real Felipe* at Callao had been enlarged and reinforced over the years, until a massive earthquake, followed by a powerful tsunami, destroyed the town and washed away most of its population in 1746. The Spanish deemed Callao of such vital importance that the city was rebuilt immediately, with the star-shaped defensive Castillo de Real Felipe overlooking the harbor. It was the single largest Spanish construction built in South America.[5] Brown, however, was not intimidated. He would blockade Callao.

After freeing prisoners on San Lorenzo Island and capturing the brig *San Pablo,* turning it into a prison and hospital ship, the *corsarios* sailed out from behind the guardian islands, and began a bombardment in Callao harbor, which, while inflicting little physical damage, shattered the nerves of the Viceroyalty, which began to realize they were not invulnerable and that it might encourage revolt from the local population as well. Trapping the merchant fleet inside the harbor did have a disruptive effect on Spanish trade. A stout defense by the pre-warned Peruvian militia and cavalry repulsed a land foray led by Captain Chitty, resulting in two dozen privateer casualties. Perhaps most significantly, over the next few weeks the *corsarios* managed to engage and capture or sink several Spanish ships, including the 464-ton, 34-gun frigate *Consecuencia,* greatly enhancing the rebel fleet. Among the prisoners captured was the newly appointed *gobernador* (governor) of Guayaquil, Brigadier Juan Manuel de Mendiburu, enroute north to Ecuador, part of the Viceroyalty of New Granada, where the *corsarios* would head next.

On February 6th, Almirante Brown ordered his brother Michael, as well as Bouchard, to remain at anchor protecting the various captured ships at the mouth of the Guayaquil estuary. Meanwhile Brown transferred to the shallower draft *Santisima Trinidad,* and accompanied by the captured *Nuestra Senora del Carmen,* made his way up the Guayas River toward the city of Guayaquil. Guayaquil had long been a favored port and one of the major Spanish shipyards, with its easy access to good quality wood. With so much wood construction, Guayaquil was subject to many fires, and the tropical climate brought on frequent epidemics. But it was also the frequent target of pirates and privateers. Brown easily battered the fort at Punta de Piedras into surrender and came within a mile of the city at Fuerte San Carlos, when he met strong resistance from half a battalion of soldiers. With the ebbing tide, the *Santisima Trinidad* was unable to turn and drifted shoreward, while soldiers waded to the stranded ship, wielding Napoleon's favorite weapon, the bayonet, with deadly results. Only Brown's threat to blow the ship's powder magazine saved his remaining crew from annihilation. The *Carmen* fled back to open waters to warn the others. Michael Brown called for immediate hostage negotiations to free his brother; Bouchard disagreed, fearing the loss of all their gains. This set the Browns and Bouchard against each other. After a confrontation that nearly turned violent, Bouchard was overruled by the other captains. It was ultimately agreed that Brown would be released in exchange for the captured new governor, the frigate *Candaleria,* three brigs and five boxes of captured correspondence from the *Consecuencia,* and that the privateers would leave Guayaquil. In the exchange, the privateers were compensated some 22,000 pesos in gold. The Viceroy Abascal decried negotiating with pirates. Deemed no longer seaworthy, the *Santisima Trinidad* was left behind. The Buenos Aires privateers sailed from Guayaquil with only four ships, the same number that had departed Buenos Aires four months before.

There was a cold hardness to Bouchard's nature. He accepted the return of his commander from captivity but felt that the family loyalty of the Brown brothers had compromised the entire mission. The small fleet regrouped in the Galapagos Islands, a volcanic archipelago straddling the equator some 600 miles west of Guayaquil. The Galapagos (Islands of the Tortoises) had long been used as a source of fresh water and base for pirates attacking the Spanish treasure ships between Lima and Panama. Whalers and fur seal hunters harvested the giant Galapagos tortoises, but the islands were uninhabited, save for the marine iguanas and other unique creatures found there. A generation later, the Galapagos Islands would be the epicenter of an intellectual earthquake with the visit of a young naturalist named Charles Darwin aboard *HMS Beagle* and the subsequent publication of his observations about the survival of the fittest and the evolution of the endemic species he encountered there.

Anchored off Charles Island, later known as Floreana, Bouchard resolved to remove himself from the strained relations with the other captains and return to Buenos Aires. In the distribution of spoils Bouchard took command of the frigate *Consecuencia,* as well as the schooner *Carmen.* Privateering was very much about the money. The two naval captains, both destined to be hailed as national maritime heroes, parted company for the last time.

Sailing back into the southern latitudes, Bouchard exchanged navigation by the Great Bear and North Star for the constellation of the Southern Cross. Residual resentment among the crew from the outward voyage grew stronger over Bouchard's conflict with the popular Irishman Brown. As a hedge against another possible mutiny, Bouchard allocated minimal supplies and the maximum number of potential dissidents to the *Carmen.* When the *Carmen* began to founder on the southward voyage toward Cape Horn and signaled that they wished to return to the Galapagos, Bouchard ignored their pleas and ordered them to continue. Insubordinate, the *Carmen* came about and remained in the Pacific. Unmoved, and possibly relieved, Bouchard continued through the southern straits. Knowing what to expect going around Cape Horn did not diminish the anxiety of the crew. After quelling another mutiny at pistol point in a duel and surviving an attempted poisoning aboard his own ship, he brought the *Consecuencia* safely to Buenos Aires on June 18, 1816.

Bouchard returned to a muted hero's welcome. His *patron* (patron) Echevarria was well pleased to now own a much bigger, more valuable ship than the one Bouchard had left on. The government applauded the boldness that had taken the new Argentine flag into the Pacific for the first time and unnerved the Spanish American Empire at its heart. But the acrimony among Bouchard's former crew would continue to cause trouble for a long time to come.

On July 9, 1816, The Congress of Tucuman formally declared the independence of the United Provinces of South America. As in colonial North America, the declaration would not end the war, but it would clarify the grievances and rationale for independence. Great Britain would be the first to recognize Argentina as an independent nation in 1825. Spain would not recognize the sovereignty of its former colony until 1863. Border disputes and fighting with her neighbors would consume Argentina for the rest of the century. Her government would be split between federalists advocating strong regional provinces and unitarians in favor of a strong centralized government. Argentina was run as a dictatorship for most of its early years until the Constitution of 1853 created the Republic of Argentina.

THAT PIRATE, BOUCHARD

Hipolito Bouchard had found his niche in the struggle as a privateer. Decades later, a boy soldier in defending Mexico in a war with the United States would utter the words, *"El mundo es de los aventados."* (The daring shall inherit the world)[6] Bouchard would have agreed. And he would sail around that world, proving it so.

Notes:

1. Sara Caputo, "Mercenary gentlemen? The transnational service of foreign quarterdeck officers in the Royal Navy of the American and French wars, 1775-1815," Historical Research, vol. 94, Issue 266, November 2021, pp. 806-826, https://doi.org/10.1093/hisres/htab028, retrieved June 22, 2022.
2. John de Courcy Ireland, "Almirante William Brown," *18th-19th Century History, Featuros,* vol. 9, issue 3, Autumn 2001, https://www.historyireland.com>almirante-william-brown, retrieved August 8, 2022.
3. N. Prieto and A. Mari, "Historia Completa de la Nacion Argentina" (Spanish ed.), Buenos Aires: vol. XXIV, 1927, p. 12.
4. Diego Barros Arana, General History of Chile, Books on Demand, 1889, pp.226-230.
5. "Fuerte del Real Felipe," 2010, https://www.starforts.com>callao, Retrieved August 9, 2022.
6. Juan Escutia, https://www.proz.com>kudoz>idioms>maxims>sayings, Retrieved August 11, 2022.

Chapter 5
Corsario

The moon shimmers on the sea
The wind moans on the canvas
And raises in soft movement
Waves of silver and blue
And sees the pirate captain
Singing happily in the stern
Asia on one side, Europe on the other.

–Jose de Espronceda y Delgado (1808-1842),
"The Pirate's Song", *Poesias* (1846).
Spanish Romantic Poem.

Celebration of Bouchard's moderate success raiding the west coast of Spanish America was short lived as a host of legal problems followed him ashore upon his return. He was summoned before a marine court of inquiry to account for a variety of charges and behavior including execution of one sailor, fighting a duel with another and the alleged callousness toward the lost *Constitucion* and its crew while crossing the Straits of Magellan. The chorus of acrimony grew even louder when the sloop *Carmen*, having been refitted in the Galapagos Islands, eventually returned to Buenos Aires under Captain Pedro Dautant. Its mutinous crew, to a man, hated Bouchard and blamed him for their mutiny. Furious with indignation, Bouchard offered defense and acquitted himself as best he could with limited resources. His relatively small share of the prize money from the ships captured off Callao barely covered his legal fees. The influence of his Merlo family relatives (Norberta was now pregnant with their second child) was diminished by the imprisonment of his wedding godfather, the former Supreme Director Posadas. His supportive officer Ramon Freire had departed for land duty with San Martin's army crossing the Andes and was unavailable (Feire would go on to become president of the young republic of Chile). The most important witness, *Almirante* Guillermo Brown was still at sea in the Pacific, though he likely would have offered only tepid support, damning Bouchard with faint praise – the two men had not parted as friends. And all of Bouchard's history: the disaffection as a *granadero,* the debacle at San Nicolas, and the indiscreet way Bouchard had alienated so many people of position were brought back up. In the end, the tribunal ruled that Bouchard was justified in his actions. The decision did not sit well with many of the crew. One evening Bouchard had to defend himself from an assassin's knife. It would not be the last attempt on his life.

With the urgency of the war with Spain, the government of the United Provinces still lacked the time and resources to fully create a regular navy. *Corsarios* such as Bouchard, Brown and others had proved effective in interrupting Spanish shipping and hampering the enemy's war effort and the government endorsed the further use of privateering. In May 1817, under the auspices of the new Supreme Director, Juan Martin de Pueyrredon, one of Bouchard's few supporters, the government formalized the terms and conditions of issuing privateer licenses, the so-called "letters of marque":

> *"The Government will grant a marque certificate to any individual who requests to arm a vessel against an enemy flag, prior to the bond that it deems appropriate before the Commissioner of the Navy, specifying in the instance the type of vessel that was intended, its bearing, weapons, supplies and staff."* [1]

Under the patronage of Vicente de Echeverria, Bouchard began the intensive refitting of the captured frigate *la Consecuencia,* which was to be renamed *la Argentina*. At 677 tons, the ship was ideal for long-distance sailing. Its 42 eight- and 12-pound guns were mounted in two batteries, along with four bronze guns in the hold and a pair of mobile cannons. Though well supplied with artillery and ammunition, there was a national shortage of available hand firearms and swords. Bouchard set about recruiting a crew which included midshipman Tomas Espora; Lt. Nathan Sommers who would serve as flag captain; 1st Lt. William Shipsi, formerly of the

British navy; and officers Daniel Oliver, Pedro Cornet, John Van Buren, Luis Geissac, Juan Harris, Miguel Borges, Carlos Douglas, and Jorge Miller. Taken on as pilots were Bouchard's two brothers-in-law, Juan Augustine and Cayetano Merlo. One hundred twenty-five infantry would also be on board under command of Captain Jose Maria Piriz of Montevideo. Many sailors refused to sail under Bouchard, given his reputation. But Buenos Aires swelled with seamen seeking work, many naval veterans of European or American wars, and the rank-and-file crew willing to sign on represented the usual mix of Argentines and foreign-born seamen.

While awaiting the privateering license, Bouchard once again came into conflict with his crew. In disciplining a crewman who had assaulted another, Bouchard was attacked with an ax. Lieutenant Nathan Sommers intervened, killing the assailant with his sword. In the melee that followed, a second sailor was killed, and several were injured before marines regained order. Another investigation ensued. This time Bouchard appealed to Pueyrredon, himself, claiming that the discontent among the crew was the result of waiting too long in port. The Supreme Director was losing patience. Hipolito Bouchard had become a thorn in the side of the ruling powers. The talented, headstrong Frenchman was as much a liability as an asset. The consensus was that he could cause the least trouble back at sea, on a voyage of great distance, and possibly dangerous, and preferably away for a long time. They would get their wish.

Thus, in June 1817, Bouchard received the coveted letter of marque, No. 116. Technically ordered to remain in port pending results of the investigation, *La Argentina* slipped up to Ensenada de Barrangan, at the mouth of the de la Plata estuary. Contrary to rumors he had fled the country, Bouchard had followed an order allowing ships to leave port in order to be more effective in open water against an attack. To use a modern analogy, he had one foot on the accelerator and one foot on the brake. On July 9th, he released the brake and sailed into open ocean. The letter of marque was to expire in sixteen months; the cruise of *La Argentina* would take them around the world and last two full years.

In legitimizing the practice of privateering, authorizing governments not only indicated a suspense date but also designated where the privateer was authorized to operate. *La Argentina* was given three options: she could return to the west coast of South America and patrol the approaches to Callao, Peru; she could wait in the lee of various Caribbean islands and intercept Spanish shipping; or she could take the fight directly to Spain and attack the bustling port of Cadiz. Now autonomous in open waters, Bouchard had other ideas. Earlier that spring another Argentine privateer had captured a Spanish ship of the Royal Company of the Philippines, *the Triton,* with an extremely valuable cargo. Bouchard set his *corso* (privateering enterprise). He would follow the money and sail to the source of that great wealth, Manila, on the far side of the globe.

Within days of departure La Argentina experienced trouble. A suspicious fire broke out onboard. There were a pair of furnaces on the ship, used for melting lead for bullets and round shot, but the fire could easily have been purposely set by a crew member. In the age of sail, fire aboard a vessel made almost entirely of wood, adrift in mid ocean, often spelled doom for both ship and crew. Mariners, prone to superstition, would treat this fire as a bad omen. *La Argentina's* crew doused the stubborn fire, as the South American current pushed the frigate toward the coast of Africa, sailing out of the Atlantic, around Cape of Good Hope, and arriving at the port of Tamatave, on the east coast of the island of Madagascar on September 4th.

In port, Bouchard encountered four ships, three British, one French, that were openly engaged in the notorious trade of human slaves. According to scholar Gwyn Campbell, the export of slaves from Madagascar to the various markets in East Africa and the western Indian Ocean had been long established, and the more recent rise of the local Merina Empire on the island had called for importation of slaves to serve the developing plantation economy on Madagascar as well[2] By the early 19th century, Great Britain was trying to stem the trans-Atlantic slave trade and was about to conclude a treaty to that effect with the ruler of Madagascar. A British officer enlisted Bouchard's assistance in blockading the port at Tamatave and freeing the slaves held on the anchored ships. With the specter of the Haitian slave rebellion burned in his memory, Bouchard gladly accommodated the request.

In his own words in correspondence to Pueyrredon,

> *"I offered him all the forces under my command and said that I would do all I could to prevent such a vile commerce, by virtue of the treaties with the European nations and the high aims of Your Excellency which are to abolish, within your reach, all forms of slavery."*[3]

In addition to setting free the captives, Bouchard appropriated the food and other supplies for his own use aboard *la Argentina* (though he did issue a receipt reimbursable in Buenos Aires).

Several freed slaves as well as five sailors from the French ship were recruited to sail with this French speaking South American. After ten days, *la Argentina* was relieved by the British corvette *Conway*, and she sailed east in search of Spanish ships to plunder.

At sea, *la Argentina* encountered an United States frigate out from the Bay of Bengal, which reported that a ship of the Royal Company of the Philippines had not been seen trading in Indian waters for over three years. Undaunted, Bouchard pressed on, skirting the Indian sub-continent and heading toward the thousands of islands of Indonesia. Storms battered the Argentine corsair and onboard Bouchard faced an even greater threat as much of the crew came down with scurvy. A deficiency of vitamin C, scurvy had debilitated sailing ships for centuries, though the British navy had established that it could be controlled by the juice of citrus fruit and a diet rich in fresh vegetables. A supply of such perishable foods was almost impossible to obtain and preserve on long sea voyages between ports. Scores of Bouchard's crew became ill, and dozens were buried at sea. Before entering the Sunda Strait separating the Indonesian islands of Sumatra and Java, Bouchard put into the deep-water anchorage afforded by Peucang Island off Java Head. There he set up tents as a makeshift hospital for the sick crewmen, while those well enough fished off the white sand beaches or ventured into the semievergreen rainforest on hunting forays. At one point he resorted to an almost medieval solution: on shore he buried sick sailors up to their necks; many died, others survived. With his crew decimated by epidemic, only Bouchard's force of will drove the *corso* on.

The narrow Sunda Strait links the Indian Ocean with the Java Sea and western Pacific. Notoriously difficult to navigate, with a shallow draught, shifting sandbanks and strong tides, the Strait had long been an important shipping route for the Dutch East India Company, connecting their "Spice Islands" with the wider world. Following dangerously inaccurate charts, Bouchard navigated past several volcanic islands and the crater of the sleeping Krakatoa[4] before sailing at last into the Pacific Ocean.

According to Pacific Ocean researcher Matt Matsuda, the spice trade had been carried to Europe since the time of the Roman Empire. The trade became dominated by Muslim merchants, Venetians and then Portuguese, following the Treaty of Tordesillas which gave Portugal territorial right along the eastward trade routes to the Pacific, opened by Vasco de Gama's voyages of discovery in the 15th century. Subsequently, Spanish navigators, in the wake of Ferdinand de Magellan's first circumnavigation of the globe, opened trade routes westward from the Americas toward the riches of Asia. In the late 16th century, Protestant traders in the Netherlands would challenge the hold of the Catholic Spanish and Portuguese in the Spice Islands. These merchants came together to form one of the earliest joint stock companies, the powerful Dutch East India Company, and backed by well-financed warships and well-armed mercenary army, the Dutch established a virtual monopoly on spice trade, with its center at Batavia (today's Jakarta) on the island of Java. By the time of Bouchard's voyage, the Dutch monopoly had been broken. Seeds and seedlings of nutmeg, cloves, mace, cinnamon, pepper and other valuable spices had been smuggled, or naturally dispersed by birds, wind and waves, and propagated in other lands. Junks from southeast Asia and merchant ships from Europe freely docked and traded in the Indonesian archipelago.[5]

By the time *La Argentina* left the Sunda Strait and entered the Pacific, Bouchard had sailed as far as the famous navigator Captain James Cook once thought it possible to go.

Writer Simon Winchester describes the Pacific as the oldest and

> *"by far the world's biggest body of water – all the continents could be contained within its borders, and*

> *there would be ample room to spare. It is the most biologically diverse, the most seismically active; it sports the planet's greatest mountains and deepest trenches; its chemistry influences the world; and the planetary weather systems are born within its boundaries."*[6]

It's unlikely Bouchard mused much about the sea beneath his hull, beyond what it would take to keep the ship afloat and on course with his depleted crew. Two score sailors had died and many more were wracked with dysentery and the effects of scurvy. The voyage had so far yielded nothing in Spanish plunder. He was confident that would change in the Philippines, and he remained fixated on the prize.

La Argentina's course took them past the tip of the Malay peninsula and the opening to the Straits of Malacca, an important passageway between Malaya (now Malaysia) and Sumatra, separating the Indian and Pacific oceans. The Straits historically had provided a sea route between China and India and was perennially disputed over by rival southeast Asian powers. It was also home waters for the notorious Malaccan pirates, where the many small islands, hidden coves and secluded harbors provided safety. Many pirates raided coastal communities in small gangs, while others operated in larger organized units. Malaccan pirates engaged in activities from terrorizing local populations to high seas criminality and their own version of privateering. Colonial powers such as the Dutch alternated between aggressively fighting these pirates and paying an extortion tribute to buy them off. In addition to the obvious danger posed by these pirates, dealing with them came at a high cost. Ironically, many of those in a life of piracy were themselves those left behind by international trade, an early form of globalization.

Two weeks out from Java, on the morning of December 7th, as it entered the Makassar Strait between Borneo and Sulawesi, *La Argentina* was followed by a small flotilla of five Malayan pirate *praos*, small outrigger vessels with a single sail and oars. Two of the *praos* had small caliber swivel guns mounted on the prow. Individually, these boats were no match for a heavily armed frigate but surrounding *La Argentina* in becalmed tropical waters like a swarm of angry mosquitoes, the pirates sought to attack from all sides and overwhelm the Argentine ship with close-in fighting. With oars, the *praos* quickly closed on the large ship to just beyond cannon range, then the lead ship moved in closely to attempt boarding. Bouchard's sailors and infantry soldiers, armed with rifles, pistols, swords and pikes prepared to repel the attack. The battle was fierce and bloody, lasting more than an hour. Seven Argentine sailors were wounded including the loyal Lieutenant Nathan Somers. In a counterattack, the praos was overwhelmed. Sensing defeat, its captain committed suicide by his own blade and drowning and several pirates followed suit, throwing themselves overboard. In a quick court martial, Bouchard judged the captured prisoners to be pirates and sentenced them to death.

In his logbook, Bouchard wrote,

> *"Sentencing of the crew…to the corresponding penalty for those who commit attempts or acts of piracy at sea, the penalty will consist of the sinking of the pirate ships dedicated to pillage. With their crew on board duly moored, by this war frigate."*
>
> –Hipolito Bouchard, Captain[7]

As *La Argentina* opened fire on the captured *praos*, the other Malayan pirates turned about and sailed away. A small number of the youngest pirates had been pressed into crew service on *la Argentina;* the remainder tightly bound in the hold of their own ship. *La Argentina* continued to bombard the captured vessel until all sunk below the surface of the Java Sea. Bouchard showed no remorse on passing the death sentences and though some had favored leniency, no one questioned his command.

Just into the new year of 1818, Bouchard left the Celebes Sea and sailed into the Sulu archipelago, negotiating the hidden coral reefs to anchor at Jolo Island, one of the many volcanic isles at the southwest tip of the Philippines. After seven harrowing months at sea, he was at last in the belly of the beast, though Jolo Island itself had never been subdued by the Spanish. The inhabitants had been converted to Islam in the 15th century and Jolo remained an independent Muslim state. For centuries, the Sulu Islands had been the center of trading, fishing, and slave trading between Malaya and the main Philippine Island of Luzon, as well as constant pirate activity. A treaty between the Sulu sultan and Spain in 1805 closed Sulu ports to enemies of the Spanish crown. Thus, as these Argentine strangers came ashore to resupply from the fertile island's bounty of cassava, coconuts and badly needed fruits, they were viewed with hostility by the native Tausugs. Bouchard anticipated trouble and had the crew armed and guns primed as night fell over *La Argentina* anchored in the lagoon. As a native boat called a *bow* stealthily slipped through the water toward the frigate and came within range, *La Argentina* issued a broadside and sent the would-be attackers back to shore. After more probing, the local chieftain decided to instead befriend these voyagers, treated them as guests, and allowed them to replenish their stores of food and water. By week's end, the rested and refreshed *corsarios* were ready for the final push to destination – Manila Bay.

The Philippines first came to the attention of the western world in 1519 when "discovered" by Ferdinand Magellan, who lost his life there. Some fifty years later, the Spanish, seeking a new western route to the Spice Islands, followed Magellan's route and claimed the islands they named the Philippines for King Philip II. Soon the Spanish superimposed their culture on the local population, already a heady admixture of religions, ethnicities and customs. With Manila as the entrepot for Asian trade, for the next two-and-a-half centuries, the famed Manila galleons sailed the Pacific between the Philippines and Acapulco on the North American coast of New Spain (now Mexico) loaded with tons of exotic, valuable Asian cargo and returning loaded with Mexican or Peruvian silver, which financed not only the global trade, but also the Philippine economy. However, by the early 19th century, political and economic upheaval convulsing Spanish America, and to some extent the activity of South American privateers, had seriously interrupted the galleon trade. Great treasure ships found themselves blockaded in port or interdicted on the high seas and captured. Cargoes, valuable ships and crews were lost at sea. Ships returned to home port with cargoes unsold. With trade and profit in steep decline, the last treasure ships between Asia and the New World sailed in 1815. As Bouchard sailed northwest along Luzon Island, he hoped – possibly prayed – the galleon trade was still viable and in port.

Manila Bay sits at the end of the shallow delta formed by the Pasig River. It is bordered on one side by a long peninsula. Some 30 miles from the opening, Spanish conquistador Miguel Lopez de Legazpi wrested the "city of water lilies," *Maynilad,* from the Malay Muslims in 1571, building a church, governor's residence, military barracks and an Augustinian convent around a *Plaza Mayor,* all inside a walled fortress called *Intramuros*, with seven gates and drawbridges that closed at night. The enclave was reserved for Spaniards and *mestizos* (mixed race Spanish). Outside, the local Filipino, Malay and Chinese population lived and worked. Facing the bay stood the imposing *Fuerte de Santiago,* named for the Spanish patron saint. The Santiago fort was heavily equipped with artillery protecting the approach from the sea. Except for a successful British attack in 1762, Manila had been the uncontested center of commerce and trade in Asia-Pacific for more than two centuries. Hipolito Bouchard sailed aggressively toward this formidable and heavily defended harbor and stopped just beyond the range of the Spanish cannons. He could see a pair of merchant ships anchored in the harbor, along with a Spanish war corvette and several smaller vessels. He had sailed half-way around the world for these prizes and he wanted them badly. But the Spaniards knew he was coming.

The ships in Manila Bay, the *San Fernando* and the *Rosel,* belonged to the Royal Company of the Philippines, chartered in 1785 by royal decree to stimulate trade among the Philippines, other Spanish colonies and the mother country in Europe directly. It was designed to complement rather than compete with the Manila-Mexico trade. Several restrictive import-export regulations were relaxed, Philippine ports were opened to other countries and Philippine products could be traded duty-free. Citizens of Manila, and ultimately foreigners could hold shares in the company, though the King of Spain held the majority interest. Believing these ships to be loaded with Chinese merchandise, as well as Philippine-produced silk, sugar, cotton and spices,[8] Bouchard waited for the Spanish response to his presence. Normally, an intruder would be lured into artillery range, or a single ship might be greeted by a massed flotilla of armed *faluccas* sailing forth to intercept the unwelcome guest at the harbor's mouth. But the Spaniards did neither. In fact, they had removed the guns from the ships to supplement the shore batteries and then settled into siege mode, hoping *La Argentina* would give up and sail away. For the next several weeks, *la Argentina* sailed back and forth across the mouth of the harbor, trying unsuccessfully to provoke the Spanish to come out and fight. In the meantime, *La Argentina* captured sixteen merchant ships and fishing vessels as they approached Manila, plundered them and scuttled them in view of the city walls. Behind those walls, the city dwellers were running low on provisions and were unable to receive resupply through the blockade. By the time the royal governor ordered his warships to break the blockade, *La Argentina* had finally given up in frustration and disgust. Bouchard, livid that he had been unable to capture his prey so close, set a course north along the Luzon coast, hoping for better hunting. (The Philippines remained within the Spanish Empire until insurrection and U.S. intervention during the Spanish-American War, after which the United States administered the islands until after World War II when the Republic of the Philippines was established with Manila as capital.)

Prowling the coastal waters off Luzon on April 9, La Argentina intercepted a Spanish merchantman brigantine inbound from the Mariana Islands. Though lightly armed, the swift, agile brig chose instead to run from the Argentine frigate and made for the harbor at Santa Cruz. With this prey within his grasp, Bouchard gave pursuit until the water became too shallow. The brig launched longboats that towed it into the harbor. Bouchard chased the brig into the harbor with officers Somers, Greissac and Van Burgen and several armed crewmen in three small boats of their own. When Lieutenant Somers reached the brig under cannon fire and musketry and collided with the larger ship, his masts became entangled with the mooring ropes, and it capsized. The Spaniards rained fire on the helpless men in the water from their deck above, killing fourteen including Somers. Five sailors were rescued but Bouchard was deeply grieved at the loss of his ever-faithful second-in-command and vowed revenge. Capturing a shallow draught schooner nearby, Bouchard outfitted it with several cannon and ordered Greissac and Oliver, with 35 sailors, to return to the brigantine in Santa Cruz harbor. The brig had been abandoned and was easily boarded.

Despite some exchange of cannon fire with the brigantine's crew now onshore, the Argentines were able to sail the captured brig out of the harbor without further incident. Bouchard's fleet had gained a second ship, paid for with a heavy human toll.

Soon a third ship was added, with the capture of a schooner headed for the northern island of Batanes, carrying the royal *situado,* essentially a payroll run. Dividing his depleted crew between the three ships, Bouchard put Lieutenant Oliver in command of the captured brig. Bouchard instructed them to rendezvous at San Ildefonso, around the northern tip of Luzon, on the island's east coast. After sailing together for several days, the small fleet became separated, reunited and then separated again. Bouchard waited at San Ildefonso as planned, however neither the brigantine nor the schooner appeared. Memories of losing *La Constitucion* in Drake's Passage years earlier returned. The ships could possibly have encountered bad weather in the typhoon-prone South China Sea, but with cynicism and simmering anger, Bouchard suspected one or both missing vessels had turned mutinous and sailed off toward Canton or Macao on their own in search of greater riches. At best, Lt. Oliver had the navigational skills to return to Buenos Aires. Doubly frustrated by the additional loss of crew and once again having his prizes slip through his fingers, Captain Bouchard faced perhaps his life's most fateful decision.

It was late May 1818, soon the anniversary of his voyage. With limited experience as a captain and a crew made up of veteran sailors, inexperienced teenage boys and freed slaves, all speaking different languages, he had sailed thousands of miles from his home port for a cause and for status and wealth. Instead, he had lost half his crew to disease, pirates and enemy hostilities. True, he had managed to close the port of Manila for more than two months and captured more than a dozen ships, but they were all scuttled at sea. He had captured two valuable prizes and now they were gone. The captain of the captured schooner at Santa Cruz had told hm the treasure galleons and Royal Company of the Philippines ships no longer made the long trans-Pacific voyages to Mexico, staying closer to home with runs to China. Fear of failure plagued the Frenchman. How could he return empty-handed and face his family, his patrons, his government? He could retrace his route through Indonesia hoping to encounter some random opportunities. He even mused, some would say hallucinated, about sailing to Saint Helena in the south Atlantic and liberating his exiled former emperor, Bonaparte, perhaps bringing him into the cause of South American freedom. Perhaps he should return to sea duty along the South American coast in support of San Martin and Bolivar in Peru. And what of those reports that Spanish ships still plied the waters between Canton and Manila, loaded with plunder, if someone was bold enough to take it? A privateer at heart, Bouchard decided to play the China card. It seemed to be the surest way he could redeem himself, and he was already in the neighborhood.

Captain Bouchard sailed northwest toward China on May 21, heading for the port of Canton at the mouth of the Pearl River Delta in Guangzhou on the Asian mainland. But his China endeavors were short-lived. A week of tempestuous storms roaring south from Formosa battered *La Argentina.* More sailors, already sick, succumbed and found eternal rest at sea. With his sails useless, Bouchard found himself at the mercy of the prevailing currents pulling him into the north Pacific, eastward away from Japan. His destiny would be back in the Americas after all.

Notes:

1. *Provisional Regulations for the Corso,* May 15, 1817, cited in “Corsair Cruise of Argentina,” https://secondwiki>crucero>corsario-de-la-argentina, retrieved Aug. 2, 2022.
2. Gwyn Campbell, “Madagascar and the Slave Trade (1810-1895),” *The Journal of African History*, vol. 22, issue 2, 1981, pp. 203-227, http://madarevues.recherches.gov.mg>IMG>pdf, retrieved Aug. 17, 2022.
3. Hipolito Bouchard, *Manuscripto de Bouchard,* 1819, Archivo General de la Nacion, Buenos Aires, quoted in Peter Uhrowczik, The Burning of Monterey, Los Gatos, CA: CYRIL Books, 2001, p. 52.
4. On August 27, 1883, a massive volcanic eruption of Krakatoa triggered a tsunami well over 100 feet high and killing an estimated 36,000 people across a wide area. While blowing itself apart, Krakatoa created another volcanic crater, Anak (son of) Krakatoa, which is still active.
5. Matt K. Matsuda, Pacific Worlds. A History of Seas, Peoples and Cultures, Cambridge: Cambridge University Press, 2012, pp.54-56, 73-79.
6. Simon Winchester, Pacific, New York: Harper Collins, 2015, p. 2-3.
7. Bouchard, op. cit.
8. “Today in Philippine History, March 10, 1785, the Real Compania de Filipinas was established,” *The Kahimyang Project,* https://kahimyang.com>kauswagan>articles, retrieved August 22, 2022.

Illustrations

French ship *Genereux* engaged with *HMS Leander* (1798).

Painting by Charles Henry Seaforth. During the failed relief of Malta, the French warship and crew, including young Andre-Paul Bouchard, were captured by the British and taken to Minorca by Thomas Cochrane.

Source: Wikipedia – Public Domain

Attack and take of the *Crete-a-Pierrot* (1802).

Original illustration by Auguste Raffet; engraving by Hebert. *Histoire de Napoleon*, M. de Norvins, 1839, p. 239. French attempts to suppress the Haitian slave revolt altered Bouchard's view of Napoleonic ambition.

Source: Wikimedia Commons

Battle of San Lorenzo.

Painting by Alberto Nassivera. As a young cavalry officer, Bouchard captured the Spanish flag and was noted for bravery by San Martin.

Source: Creative Commons (BY-SA3.0)

Portrait of Admiral William Brown (1825).

From a miniature by Henry Herve. The Irish-born admiral and Bouchard raided the west coast of South America before parting in disagreement.

Source: Wikimedia Commons

Frigata la Argentina.

Painting by Emilio Biggeri (1907-1977).

Source: Wikipedia

Kamehameha the Great, King of the Sandwich Islands (c. 1816).

Anonymous Chinese copy of drawing by Ludwig Choris (1795-1828). The Hawaiian king, shown in western sailor's clothing, was possibly the first foreign monarch to recognize the new nation of United Provinces of *Rio de la Plata* (Argentina). Original at Boston Athenaeum.

Source: Wikimedia Commons

Portrait of Peter Corney by unknown artist.

Corney met Bouchard in Hawai'i and inspired him to raid Alta California. Corney's writings are a major source of information about the Bouchard voyage.

Source: Wikimedia Commons

Russian Orthodox chapel at Fort Ross, California.

Fort Ross was the southernmost expansion of Russian territory in North America.

Source: Library of Congress – Public Domain

Presidio de Monterey (1791).

Etching by Jose Cardero. Original in Museo Naval, Madrid. The Presidio would be sacked and burned by Bouchard' s raiders in 1818.

Source: Wikimedia Commons

San Carlos Cathedral, Monterey, California.

Part of the original Presidio, the church was spared by Bouchard and is still in use today.

Source: Author's photograph

Bouchard at Refugio (c. 1929).

Painted wall hanging by Theodore Van Cina (1865–1940). Artist's view of the pillage of the Ortega hacienda.

Source: Santa Barbara County Courthouse Legacy Foundation/Author's photograph

Portrait of Captain Jose de la Guerra, c. 1850, by Leonardo Barbieri (1818–1896).

Defensive action by de la Guerra probably saved lives at Santa Barbara and San Juan Capistrano during the Bouchard pirate raids of 1818.

Source: Santa Barbara Trust for Historic Preservation – Public Domain

Mission San Juan Capistrano (c. 1809).

Painting by unknown artist.

Source: San Juan Capistrano Historical Society

Old Stone Church, Mission San Juan Capistrano.

Destroyed by earthquake in 1812, the original structure witnessed Bouchard's raiders' drunken spree and was never fully restored.

Source: Author's photograph

Engraving of Thomas Cochrane, 10th Earl of Dundonald.

Based on a painting by James Ramsay (1786–1854). Engraver: John Cook. Published in 1866 by London: Richard Bentley. The greatest naval officer of his day. Cochrane would be the nemesis of Hipolito Bouchard.

Source: Wikipedia – Public Domain

Guayaquil Conference between Jose de San Martin and Simon Bolivar.

Illustration by J. Collingnon (1776–1863). Following the dramatic meeting, San Martin abruptly retired and left Bolivar to complete the liberation of Peru.

Source: Wikipedia – Public Domain

Memorial bust of Bouchard, Buenos Aires.

Source: Photograph courtesy of Gary Spradlin

Portrait of Hipolito Bouchard (1835).

Painting by Jose Gil de Castro (1785–1840). Original in the collection of Eduardo Huart, Santiago.

Source: Wikimedia Commons – Public Domain

Chapter 6
Privateers in Paradise

"The loveliest fleet of islands that lies anchored in any ocean."

–Mark Twain, describing Hawai'i,
Sacramento Union, 1866

"E na'I wale no oukou, I ku'u pono 'a' ole pau (Continue my righteous deeds, they are not yet finished)."

–King Kamehameha I, last words, 1819

Long before Vasco Nunez de Balboa saw it from Darien on the Isthmus of Panama; long before Ferdinand Magellan sailed into it and named it; perhaps a millennium before any Europeans encountered the Pacific Ocean, early Polynesian sailors, using only the stars and their knowledge of the wind and waves, completed the most extraordinary navigation in history. These early seafarers sailed their double hulled canoes out from the Marquesas, across the entire Pacific, making landfall in the north of that vastness on an isolated volcanic archipelago we have come to call Hawai'i.

Successive waves of these intrepid voyagers brought their families, flora and fauna to these islands, establishing a community and culture insulated from the rest of the known – or unknown – world. Ambiguous records suggest a Spanish fleet under Ruy Lopez de Villalobos may have come across the Hawaiian Islands in 1542 while sailing between Acapulco and Manila. However, for reasons of state security, the route of the Spanish treasure galleons was kept secret and they traversed the ocean between America and the Philippines with the prevailing North Pacific current well north of the Hawaiian chain, allowing Hawai'i to remain independent of any foreign powers intent on claiming new territory.

It was not until the voyages of British explorer James Cook, the greatest navigator of his day, that Hawai'i became known to the outside world. After verifying the existence of the Great Southern Continent (Antarctica), Captain Cook was sent to the other polar region to look for the long-sought Northwest Passage between the North Atlantic and North Pacific. Unable to find such a sea route, (it didn't exist, although 21st century global warming may make it a reality after all) Cook sailed from Alaska back into the wide Pacific and made his second visit to Hawai'i in 1779 (In a dispute over a stolen longboat and disrespect of some local religious customs, Cook was killed on the shore of the island of Hawai'i). But publication of the accounts of Cook's visits had awakened interest in these overlooked islands, which he had called the Sandwich Islands in honor of his patron, the 4th Earl of Sandwich. Soon traders, whalers and later missionaries, would arrive in great numbers from many nations, bringing disease and the clash of cultures, but also bringing Hawai'i into the world of global trade.

Following the American War of Independence, American whalers and merchants needed to seek alternative markets from Britain. They sailed around the Horn in great numbers, bound for the now-open port of Canton. Trade with Hawai'i followed shortly. Hawai'i became a regular port-o-call for ships sailing between the Pacific northwest and China.[1]

Each of the larger Hawaiian Islands was ruled independently by kings and chieftains, or *ali'is.* The king of the big island of Hawai'i had been waging war with the other islands for more than a decade when Captain George Vancouver, an important explorer in his own right and who had sailed with Captain Cook, arrived in Hawai'i in 1792. King Kamehameha I appraised the firepower of the British warships and petitioned the British for protection. Britain, more interested in alliances for trade than in claiming new territory, agreed, enabling King Kamehameha to unite the other islands under his rule by 1795 (Kauai Island was subjugated much later.) Although the alliance was never formally ratified, the Union Jack was incorporated into the Hawaiian flag and remains part of the Hawai'i state flag today.

King Kamehameha established a constitutional monarchy based on European models. He set about modernizing his kingdom, while still retaining many of the centuries-old practices of *taboo,* thus maintaining the power of the *kahunas* (priests) and the *ali'i* aristocracy. As the Sandwich Kingdom opened to trade, thousands of young *kanakas* (Hawaiian men) sailed out on foreign ships and returned with useful intelligence about the world. With profits from sandalwood trade, import duties and harbor taxes, Kamehameha began assembling his own small merchant fleet.

According to Matt Matsuda,

> *"Monarchical interests in foreign trade made Hawai'i open to rapid developments in the building of wharves and shipyards. Boarding houses, saloons and brothels clustered along waterfronts and livestock and produce were carted from inland to harbors, creating a cash economy tying villages to semi-permanent whaling settlements."* [2]

In mid-August 1818, an unfamiliar ship under an unfamiliar flag dropped anchor in Kealakekua Bay, the port for Karakakowa, Kamehameha's capital on the big island of Hawai'i. The corvette had sloppily repainted the name on the stern and called itself *Victory*. The ship's captain was an Englishman, Jose (Joseph) Turner but the unruly crew were mainly Spanish-speaking and wasted no time hurrying ashore and spending wildly like the proverbial drunken sailors they were. The free-flowing gold and silver coin, along with the cache of valuable religious objects on board, quickly raised suspicions that the *Victory* was not as represented.

In fact, this visiting ship was a Philadelphia-built corvette in the service of the United Provinces of the Rio de la Plata as a privateer. It was owned by Rafael Pereyra Lucena. Originally named *Liberty,* it had sailed as *la Libertad*, before being renamed *Santa Rosa de Chacabucco,* in celebration of General San Martin's great victory. Sheathed in copper and armed with four long 12-pounders, two short 12-pounders and eight 18-pound cannonades, and a crew of 135 men, she had set sail from Buenos Aires about a month before *la Argentina.* Months later, while privateering off the coast of Valparaiso, Chile, the crew had mutinied, put the officer cadre ashore, and sailed away to engage in pure piracy. A Chilean commodore vowed to find and destroy the ship. On a course for Hawai'i, the mutineers had renamed the ship *Victory,* in a vain attempt to disguise her identity and avoid capture.

According to oral tradition. King Kamehameha had received a cargo of Chinese silk and Indonesian rum, or arrack, on his own brig, the *Forester* (*Kaahumanu* in Hawaiian), after its captain, Alexander Adams, traded expensive Hawaiian sandalwood in Canton. Because gold was unknown on Hawai'i and the pirates needed silver to exchange for provisions on the *Santa Rosa,* Captain Adams willingly exchanged silver for the Spanish gold at a par exchange rate, resulting in a huge profit to himself and the king. Meanwhile, Kamehameha sold the rum to the pirates at grossly inflated price. When the pirates had drained all the rum and the king had drained all the silver from their purses, Kamehameha purchased *the Victory/Santa Rosa* with the pirates' own silver. Another name change followed, *Liholiho,* and Captain Adams prepared to fit the ship for a voyage to Canton. But before the *Liholiho* could embark, another ship sailed into Kealakekua Bay: *la Argentina.*[3]

It took Captain Bouchard scant time to recognize the ship as the *Santa Rosa de Chacabucco.* Had Bouchard sailed around South America he would have joined up with her off Chile. The *Santa Rosa* had carried privateer marque no. 88. Meanwhile the pirate crew had dispersed throughout the islands. Some had already taken Hawaiian wives. Most of the ringleaders of the mutiny had fled to Kauai Island, outside the realm of Kamehameha. Captain Turner had already left from Honolulu on board a ship bound for Canton.

Bouchard's famous fury boiled over. He demanded a meeting with King Kamehameha and produced a document ordering the seizing of the *Santa Rosa* and the punishment of its mutinous crew. The letter was designed to legitimize ships sailing on behalf of the new Argentine government. Through an American interpreter, Don Juan de Eliot y Castro (John Elliot), Bouchard explained the crew to be mutineers and pirates who had pillaged churches as well as plundered ships on the high seas. The king agreed and ordered the capture of the sailors in question. Like the great Polynesian fishermen they were, the Hawaiians cast a wide net and in short order captured most all the pirate crew still on Hawai'i. The king then demanded compensation for the *Santa Rosa* and the expenses incurred by the prisoners. Bouchard agreed to compensate the cost of the sandalwood cargo.[4] In addition Bouchard presented Kamehameha with a sword, his naval hat, uniform and commission as a lieutenant colonel of the United Provinces. There is little evidence Bouchard had authority to do any of this.

In a manuscript, *la Argentina's* infantry officer, Jose Maria Piriz, writes:

> *"We celebrate a union treaty for peace, war and trade, the King being obliged with this to send to the disposal of our supreme government all the ships that arrive from these coasts, such as La Chacabucco, and to give us men and aid, as many as asked for our help, recognizing since then our independence."* [5]

Scholars differ on whether the signed agreement between commodore and king constitutes a formal treaty. Some claim this represents the first official recognition of the sovereignty of Argentina by a foreign power. Others believe it was the Frenchman's clever way to gain control of *the Santa Rosa* and exact punishment on its mutinous crew, who to Bouchard were deserving of death.

Historian Lewis H. Bealer suspects that Bouchard may have had this intention from his first glimpse of *Santa Rosa.*

> *"To avoid any question as to his own authority to act in this manner, Bouchard very blandly presented to King Kamehameha a forged document which purported to be a formal order from the government of Buenos Aires, dated 27 April 1818, instructing Bouchard to hunt down the Santa Rosa wherever it might be found."*

Dated in April, when Bouchard was still sailing the waters around the Philippines, the letter could not have originated in Buenos Aires.[6]

While Bouchard, at all times, acted with great formality and deference to the king, privately he considered the Hawaiians little more than naïve savages.

Following an examination of existing archival records, scholar Robert Lydecker concluded,

> *"That Captain Bouchard was authorized to make treaties is in itself doubtful. There are papers in the archives authorizing all of his actions while here [Hawai'i], but there are none giving him power to make treaties, and it is extremely doubtful that he had such power. That the first treaty [between Hawai'i and another sovereign power] was made with the United States, during Capt. Jones' visit in 1826, there is no doubt."* [7]

Nevertheless, with the completion of negotiations, Bouchard took command of the *Santa Rosa*. It would require weeks to repair her damage, ensure her to be seaworthy, reinstall the guns that had been off-loaded, and re-provision her for sea duty. After fourteen months, Hipolito Bouchard now commanded a second ship as well.

If vengeance is the Lord's, Bouchard was his avenging angel. Not only had Bouchard assumed responsibility for bringing the mutineers to trial, but he simply viewed their actions as an affront to all ship captains' authority, and his moral outrage was reinforced by his own personal experiences with mutinous crews. On September 6th, he began a sweep of the other islands to locate the remaining fugitives. On Molokai, they apprehended nineteen more sailors from the *Santa Rosa.* Bouchard assumed the role of Argentine diplomat at large. At the whaling port of Lahaina, on Maui Island, Bouchard took it upon himself to appoint an American, Edmund Butler, as Argentine consul. However, discrepancies in the signatures suggest the documentation was not official or even authentic.[8] At Honolulu, on Oahu Island, he made a similar appointment of Francisco de Paula de Marin, a Spaniard acting as counselor to the king, again without authority from the United Provinces.[9] It was also in Honolulu that Bouchard encountered Peter Corney, who would play a major role in the coming months.

Peter Corney was an English officer aboard the Northwest Company's fur trader *Columbia.* The *Columbia* had made several voyages across the Pacific between the Columbia River in North America and the ports of Canton and Macau, stopping several times in the Sandwich Islands to refit and replenish supplies. In late 1817, The *Columbia* sailed to Hawai'i and was offered for sale to King Kamehameha, who agreed on the price of two cargoes of sandalwood. Corney would later write an account of his adventures, titled *Voyages in the Northern Pacific. Narrative of several trading voyages from 1813 to 1818, between the northwest coast of America, the Hawaiian Islands and China, with a description of the Russian establishments on the northwest coast. Interesting early account of Kamehameha's realm; manners and customs of the people etc. And a sketch of a cruise in the service of the independents of South America in 1819.*

Corney describes his encounter with Bouchard:

> *"[Bouchard] brought both ships down to Woahoo [Oahu] to refit. On their arrival, Captain Bouchard came to our houses, where he spent most of his time, often inviting us on board. He took a particular fancy to me and asked me to command the Santa Rosa, to which I agreed, and in October 1818, entered on my office. We sailed for Atooi [Kauai], to take on board some of the Santa Rosa's mutineers, who had been left there by the brig, and got four of them, but could not find Mr. Griffiths (ringleader Enrique Griffiths). The Commodore being determined to shoot him, told Tamooree (local king Kaumualii) that if the man was not produced, he would destroy the fort and set fire to the village. Three days after Griffiths was sent in a prisoner, tried by a court martial, and sentenced to be shot, having but two hours to make his peace with the Almighty. He was brought down to the beach (where the Patriot colors were displayed) blindfolded and shot by four marines belonging to the Argentina."* [10]

Corney goes on to describe Bouchard's relentless pursuit of any remaining mutineers, finding four more on Oahu, then sailing next to Maui Island, where he hired locals to flush the fugitives out of the mountains and the slopes of Haleakala crater. Within days, all crew from the *Santa Rosa* that had not fled the Hawaiian Islands altogether were gathered for court martial. One was sentenced to be shot but reprieved. The others received the harsh sentence of twelve dozen lashes, and the punishment was meted out under Bouchard's gaze, his stern countenance unmoved.[11]

Hipolito Bouchard listened with interest to Peter Corney's descriptions of trading along the coast of North America. He was intrigued by the presence of the Russians as far south as Alta California. The Russians were also trying to establish a foothold on Kauai and had denied Bouchard putting ashore there on his manhunt for fugitives. But Bouchard was mainly interested in knowledge of Spanish California. Were there riches to be had? Did the Spanish treasure ships sail California waters? Were the people of Mexico revolting against their Spanish overlords as well? As on a rising tide, Bouchard's spirits were lifted. He now had two large, well-fitted warships under his command. And his level of self-importance had never been higher, having imbued himself with plenipotentiary powers of full diplomatic authority. He would return to the Americas and enrich himself on the way home.

Before leaving the Hawaiian Islands, Bouchard recruited more mariners to augment his depleted crew, including a large complement of Sandwich Islanders, along with Americans, Spaniards, Portuguese, Creoles, Negroes, Malays, "Manila men" (Filipinos), and a few Englishmen such as Peter Corney. One account has a bevy of Hawaiian women also making the voyage, though no further mention of this is found.

Peter Corney writes:

> *"The ships then made sail for Woahoo (Oahu) where we took on board a supply of hogs and vegetables and a number of natives; and on the 20th of October we took our leave of those friendly natives, bound for the coast of California, to cruise against the Spaniards."* [12]

Corney continues,

> *"On our passage towards California we were employed exercising the great guns, and putting the ship in good condition for fighting, frequently reading the articles of war which are very strict and punish with death almost every act of insubordination."* [13]

One detail during the cruise toward California that Bouchard either overlooked, ignored or rationalized away was the fact that his letter of marque, his privateer's license, had reached its expiration date. Henceforth he could be considered a common pirate. History doesn't provide the inner workings of the Commodore's mind on the issue. He was still thousands of miles from his South American home base with no way to communicate. One can only guess the lure of sacking a Spanish capital was too great and would hopefully grant him an extension after the fact. Headstrong to a fault, he found the North Pacific current that pushed him toward the Oregon coast of North America, then sailed south, putting in first at Fort Ross, (as recounted in Chapter 1).

Notes:

1. S.E. Morrison, "Boston Traders in the Hawaiian Islands 1789-1823," *The Washington Historical Quarterly*, vol. 12, no. 3, July, 1921, p. 167, https://journals.lib.washington.edu, retrieved Aug. 31, 2022.
2. Matt Matsuda, Pacific Worlds. A History of Seas, Peoples and Cultures, Cambridge: Cambridge University Press, 2012, p. 154.
3. William DeWitt Alexander, "Captain Bouchard and the Spanish Pirates," *The Friend,* Honolulu, HI, vol. 49, no. 3, March 1891, p. 18, Originally published in *Maile Wreath.*
4. When distilled, the aromatic oils of sandalwood fetched very high prices in the market at Canton and beyond. Long used in Asia for perfume, cosmetics and incense, sandalwood was an important Hawaiian export until the forests were depleted in the 19th century. It sold for as much as $10 per picul (133 lbs.).
5. Jose Maria Piriz, *Manuscript,* 1819, Archivo Mitre, Armario 1, box 16, Buenos Aires.
6. Lewis W. Bealer, "Bouchard in the Islands of the Pacific," *Pacific Historical Review*, vol. 4, no. 4, Dec. 1935, p. 339.
7. Robert C. Lydecker, "The Archives of Hawaii," *Papers of the Hawaiian Historical Society*, n. 13, Honolulu HI, 1906, p. 13, http://hdl.handle.net/10524/979, retrieved Aug. 27, 2022.
8. "The Recognition of Don Eduardo Butler as Agent of the Government of the United Provinces", 11 September 1818, Hawai'i State Archives, Foreign Office and Executive Records, 1790-1900, Box 402-2-9, Chronological File 1790-1849.

9. Francisco de Paula Marin (1774-1831) became the unofficial diplomatic corps of the Hawaiian Kingdom, maintaining good relations with envoys from many nations. A Spanish seaman who had deserted on Hawai'i, he acted as an interpreter, military advisor and royal physician to King Kamehameha I. As a horticulturist, he is credited with introducing cultivation of the pineapple, orange, mango and cotton to the islands. He produced the first wine grapes, distilled brandy and made rum from sugar cane. More than a year after he left Hawai'i, Bouchard would write to Don Marin, inquiring about a pirated brigantine, instructing Marin to seize it and sell it on behalf of its owners.

10. Peter Corney, Voyages in the Northern Pacific, Honolulu, HI: Thos. G. Thrum, Publisher, 1896, pp. 119-120. Reprinted from *The London Literary Gazette* of 1821.

11. Ibid.

12. Ibid.

13. Ibid.

Chapter 7

Ese Pirata Buchar [1]

"It is the California that men dreamed of years ago, this is the Pacific that Balboa looked at from the peak of Darien, this is the face of the earth as the creator intended it to look."

–Henry Miller, *Big Sur and the Oranges of Hieronymus Bosch,* 1957 [2]

"Monterey, as far as my observation goes, is decidedly the pleasantest and most civilized-looking place in California."

–Richard Henry Dana, Jr., *Two Years Before the Mast. A Sailor's Life at Sea, 1840*

November 1818. Now supplied with eggs, vegetables and fresh water, *la Argentina* and *Santa Rosa* left the Fort Ross harbor at Rumiantsev (modern Bodega Bay), skirted the seal colony on the rocky Farallon islands and glided past the totally fog-obscured gateway to San Francisco Bay on their port side. A small group of Costanoan Native Americans scarcely paid attention to the shapes barely visible on the horizon as they stood knee-deep one morning in the shallow pools among the rocks created by the minus tide. They were too intent on prying the abalone from the exposed rocks, the iridescent bowl-shaped shells as prized as the succulent mollusk meat tightly attached to the shell's underside. These natives, neophytes attached to the Franciscan mission at Santa Cruz a few miles south on the northern rim of Monterey Bay, were harvesting the plentiful shellfish just as their ancestors had done for centuries. And besides, the sight of billowed sails on passing sailing ships had become a more common sight, unlike for those ancestors who thought the sailing ships of the first bearded Europeans to explore the California coast were giant sea birds.

Not long after the Spanish conquest of the Aztec Empire and the establishment of the viceroyalty of *Nueva Espana* (New Spain, comprising modern Mexico, parts of the United States, and a portion of Central America), the Spanish instituted the annual voyages of the Manila Galleons between the Mexican port of Acapulco and the Philippines. Because the North Pacific current brought the galleons back to America in a clockwise rotation, the course brought them far north of Acapulco, and the Spanish government hoped to find a suitable safe port along the north coast of Alta California where the galleons could resupply and repair before sailing down the coast to Acapulco. The exploration fell to Juan Rodriguez Cabrillo, a naval commander who had played a major role in the conquest of the Aztec capital – now Mexico City. Although Cabrillo discovered the bay he called *Bahia de los Pinos* (Bay of the Pines) in 1542, he did not land and explore around the crescent coastline between Santa Cruz and Point Pinos. Instead, he sailed on to the north, somehow missing the entrance to San Francisco Bay. Upon return, Cabrillo died from an injury on the Channel Islands off Santa Barbara. His reports about Monterey Bay were forgotten. It would be half a century before Sebastian Rodriguez Cermeno, returning from Manila, called the location *Bahia de San Pedro* (Bay of St. Peter). Cermeno met with disaster ashore and never followed up. Ultimately, the merchant Captain Sebastian Vizcaino, a former Manila trader, charted the coast some 2,000 miles from Cabo San Lucas to Cape Mendocino. By December 1602, he reached the large bay previously described by Cermeno. Believing the bay to be ideal for the galleon fleet, with abundant pine and other wood for ship building and repair, he named it *Puerto de Monterrey* (Port of Monterrey) in honor of the current governor of New Spain, Don Gaspar de Zuniga y Acevedo, the 5th Count of Monterrey (Monterrei in Galicia, Spain). But again, plans to establish a port at Monterey were set aside as too remote, too dangerous, too expensive. Instead, the Spanish focused on a northern Pacific Island haven for the galleons on Guam. Although the Spanish would not establish a presence in Alta California for another 160 years, the name stuck and the bay henceforth was known as Monterrey (the original Spanish spelling used the double letter *rr,* which was rolled when pronounced. This text will use the single *r* spelling to avoid confusion).

In the end, it was neither fear of English privateers nor the search for a suitable, safe deep-water harbor for their galleons that moved Spain to colonize Alta California. Rather, it was increased interest by other nations, particularly Britain, in the northwest of America, and most particularly the incursion of Russian fur traders and trappers south as far as the great bay at San Francisco. Thus, the Spanish monarch, Carlos III, ordered a strategy for protecting the northern reaches of his far-flung colonial empire. The plan was to establish a chain of missions, supported and protected by strategically placed *presidios* (forts) along the coast of California. The venture would begin at San Diego and then proceed north to Monterey.

Short of military personnel in *Nueva Espana* and equally strapped for cash, the government turned to the church for help. The Catholic Jesuit order of priests had followed the Spanish conquistadors to the New World and quickly established missions in New Spain and South America. Fearing their growing power and influence worldwide, the Spanish crown expelled the Jesuits from the Americas in 1767. They were replaced by the Franciscan order. The reformist Visitor General in Mexico City, Jose de Galvez, called on Franciscan friar Junipero Serra, recently arrived at San Blas in Baja (Lower) California, to take over the former Jesuit operations and extend them into Alta (Upper) California. *Father-Presidente* Serra had formed a partnership with Captain Gaspar de Portola, military governor in Baja California. Together they were charged by Galvez to spread the Catholic faith, thwart foreign expansion and further Spanish claim to Alta California.

In 1769, Portola led a thousand-mile land expedition north from San Diego, discovering a vast bay at San Francisco. However, he either missed or failed to recognize the Bay of Monterey. A second trek, comprised of a mule train and herd of cattle, driven by twenty mounted Spanish soldiers and several Christianized Native Americans made a return reconnoiter and this time found the *Bahia de Monterrey*. Serra and others arrived on the ship *San Antonio,* shortly thereafter. On June 3, 1770, the *Presidio* of Monterey and the second Alta California mission (the first was at San Diego) called Mission San Carlos Borromeo were established. (The following year, the mission would be moved to nearby Carmel). Monterey would be the capital of Alta California under Spanish, and later Mexican, rule until the Bear Flag Revolt and annexation of California by the United States in 1846.

The survival of the California *presidios* and missions depended upon the labor provided by the indigenous population. The story of the treatment of the native Californians in the mission system is a tragic one. But in 1768, as Elias Castillo writes,

> *"Along Alta California's coast, indigenous people went about their daily tasks, fishing, gathering clams on the beaches, checking their stores of acorns and other foodstuffs gathered for the winter, and tending fires for warmth and cooking. California's Indians were blissfully unaware that the Spaniards were preparing to seize their lands and violently end their way of life."* [3]

Nineteen missions followed, forming a chain from San Diego in the south to Sonoma north of San Francisco Bay, abutting Russian occupied territory and Fort Ross. In addition to San Diego and Monterey, *presidios* were also established at San Francisco and Santa Barbara to protect the missions. The mission communities were designed to be self-sufficient from the start. Exploiting native labor, virtually enslaved in the name of Christ, the missions planted fruit trees, olives, vegetables, grains and vineyards. They learned to make everything they needed, and they willingly traded with passing Yankee and other trading ships, or neighboring Russians, for anything they couldn't manufacture themselves, despite an official Spanish mercantile ban on trade other than with the mother country. Perhaps the greatest success of the missions was the development of large herds of cattle, horses and other livestock, as well as the associated industries such as tallow and hides. Mission life was not idyllic as it would later be romanticized in fiction and song. Conflict among the church properties, lay community and the military in the *presidios* was common. Indian revolt, despite severe repressive measures taken by the friars, was a constant threat. But the colonization of Alta California did endure and even thrived at times. The population increased, and the Spanish immigrants became less dependent upon New Spain and more independent of its governance. At the same time, Spain's grip on this outpost of empire was loosening, as Madrid's treasury was drained by European wars, the treasure galleons interrupted by South American *independistas,* and limited military personnel redeployed to the insurgencies in Mexico, South America or to the Napoleonic wars on the continent.

The original *presidio* at Monterey consisted of living quarters, a storehouse, and a small adobe church with bell tower. The buildings were enclosed by a palisade of earth and pine logs, eventually approximately 200 feet square. Cannons were mounted at each corner. Outside the palisade, pens corralled livestock and a powder magazine and guardhouse were constructed. However, from the beginning, the *presidio* was considered inadequate for defense, and its conditions quickly deteriorated. When British explorer Captain George Vancouver observed the Monterey presidio in 1792 and 1793, he found it totally unprepared for an enemy attack. Over the ensuing years, the *presidio* was tripled in size, but its condition did not improve. Earthquakes, fire, log-rot, and poor foundational construction all took their toll. By 1778, the log and earth stockade was converted to a stone and adobe construction. In 1792, a gun emplacement, *El Castillo,* was constructed, overlooking the harbor. Cannons were relocated there from the *presidio,* which no longer served as a fort. Vancouver noted the small guard of Spanish soldiers living there in wretched huts. The *presidio* remained the center of local administration and most of the residents lived within its damp, unsanitary walls. Unlike the missions that seemed to get wealthier, the *presidio* remained dependent on the annual arrival of the supply ship from San Blas, Mexico. But the ship's arrival became less dependable, and trade with ships from other countries was sporadic. Monterey became a nearly forgotten military outpost rather than a town.

By 1815, when Peter Corney, later of the *Santa Rosa* with Bouchard, made his first visit to Monterey, he observed:

> *"The town of Monterey is most pleasantly situated on a beautiful and extensive plain, and nearly half a mile from a sandy beach. It consists of about 50 houses of one story built in a square, surrounded by a stone wall, about 18 feet high, on the south side of the square stands the church, on the west the governor's house;*

> *and on the east side the lieutenant governor's house and king's stores; on the north side is the grand and principal entrance, a gaol [sic] and guardhouse and in the middle are two field pieces, 6 pounders. There are many farmhouses scattered over the plain, with large herds of cattle and sheep; on the north side of the bay is the river Carmel, which is full of excellent salmon and other fish. The fort stands on a hill, about one mile to the westward of the town."* [4]

As for the population of Monterey, he wrote,

> *"The governor and a few others are old Spaniards; the remaining inhabitants are Creoles of the country. They keep the Indians under great subjection, making them work very hard, chained two and two, the whole population of Monterey does not exceed 400 souls...Two ships touch here annually for tallow and to bring supplies for the establishments on California."* [5]

From the first exploration, the population of Alta California was destined to be mixed ethnically and socially. "One third of men and one quarter of women who founded San Jose and San Francisco in 1777 called themselves *espanoles* [Spaniards], but no one inquired too closely into what the name meant."[6] Although it offered steady employment and some retirement benefits, military posting to California was not a sought-after assignment. Military pay, when available, was low and so was morale. Spanish officers often disdained the mixed-race soldiers, and the soldiers constantly ran afoul of the moral police – the mission fathers – who objected to their gambling, drinking and attention to the native women. The soldiers were ill-equipped and often bored and reduced to laborers rather than soldiering. By 1790, many of the Spanish officers, the *peninsulares,* had been recalled to Spain in the wake of the French Revolution, causing a leadership vacuum in far-away California. Many soldiers resented having to enforce the harsh treatment of the mission Indians. Instead, many soldiers were essentially customs officials, policing the coast for smugglers and pretending to enforce the royally decreed no-foreign-trade policies. The Spanish were not only concerned with the illegal trade, but also that the open trade would yield intelligence to another nation, i.e. the United States or Russia, that could aid them in an attack on Alta California. By the mid 1810s, strict enforcement of prohibition on fur trapping and foreign trade greatly curtailed foreign access to Spanish ports. But paranoia ran deep; Spanish authorities fully understood how vulnerable their *presidios* and mission properties were. Secure for nearly three centuries, Spanish America was now weakened and susceptible as prey.

In his research on the Spanish military in California, B.E. Malcolm concluded,

> *"Without the aid of intimidating bastions for protection California's small military contingent was fortunate in not being seriously challenged for control of the province...In many ways the presidios and castillos were symbolic of the entire Spanish effort in California. Small and under-manned they served primarily to establish a presence in New Spain's last frontier that, although weak, proved to be adequate in maintaining royal control."*[7]

That sense of security would be soon shattered as the frigate *la Argentina* and the corvette *Santa Rosa de Chacabucco* sailed through the forming fog bank off the San Mateo coast with a heading due south-southeast to Monterey Bay on the afternoon of November 20, 1818.

They were not unexpected. Bouchard planned to enter Monterey Bay by deceit, disguising the true nationality of his ships and taking the port by surprise. He was unaware that, weeks earlier, the Spanish had received advance warning of his arrival and had time to prepare their defenses. While in Hawai'i, Bouchard had enlisted the aid of the 150-ton, six-gun American schooner *Clarion,* in his efforts to secure the mutineers harbored on Kauai. The *Clarion* skipper, Captain Henry Gyzelaar, overheard the *independistas*' plans to attack Alta California and sailed away from Hawai'i several days before *la Argentina* left Honolulu. Gyzelaar sailed quickly to Santa Barbara, where he had established a trading relationship with the *presidio* commander, Jose de la Guerra, and had a shipment of arms to deliver. The Spanish of Alta California had heard rumors of privateers for years. Now aware of the real pending threat from the sea, de la Guerra reinforced his own position and notified the royal governor, Pablo Vicente Sola, in Monterey. De la Guerra also sent messages to the other missions and the two other *presidios* at San Diego and San Francisco to be on alert.

The lag time allowed by Bouchard's later departure from Hawai'i and his stay at Fort Ross allowed Governor Sola to effect a mass evacuation of civilians from Monterey, transporting anything of value, including the governmental archives, household goods and religious objects and art from the church. Livestock were herded to Rancho del Rey near Salinas and the populace dispersed as far away inland as Mission Soledad. Many of the Native Americans scattered into the surrounding hills. Their small garrison of two score Spanish soldiers under the command of Sergeant Manuel Gomez, including an improvised shore battery under Corporal Jose Jesus Vallejo, remained to defend the *presidio* against Bouchard's combined crew of nearly 400 sailors and militia. It was too late to heed decades of warnings about being too lightly defended.

The lookout at Point Pinos, about three miles west of the *presidio* on the tip of the Monterey Peninsula, spotted the approaching ships and raised the alarm. Bouchard stayed safely becalmed at sea in deeper water on board *la Argentina,* while the shallower draught *Santa Rosa,* flying a false American flag, was pulled into the bay by sailors rowing the longboats.

Corney writes,

> *"Being well acquainted with the bay I ran in and came too [sic] at midnight, under the fort; the Spaniard hailed me frequently to send a boat on shore, which I declined."* [8]

The ruse had failed. Wanting to attack under cover of darkness, Bouchard next sent sailors from *la Argentina* to supplement those on *Santa Rosa* in a night attack on land led by William Sheppard. To Bouchard's fury, the sailors, exhausted from pulling their ship with ropes by rowing, failed to land that night and instead waited until morning.

Now twice frustrated, Bouchard could only watch from offshore as the *Santa Rosa* engaged in an artillery duel at dawn with the shore battery on *El Castillo*. In the age of sail, gun battles between ships and shore fortifications were generally to be avoided. The ship's cannons had trouble adjusting to the elevation of the shore guns, while the Spanish artillery managed to score several hits on the *Santa Rosa,* damaging the ship and killing or wounding several sailors. Unable to maneuver out of range, Corney, now flying the flag of Argentina, struck her colors and the sailors abandoned ship in longboats and rowed back to *la Argentina.* Round one to the Spanish. After another salvo from shore, three sailors who had remained on board the *Santa Rosa* surrendered and came ashore as prisoners.

Bouchard recorded,

> *"After seven rounds of fire I saw with disgust our flag being lowered and people escaping in boats toward my ship."*

While the Spanish paused to enjoy their spirited defense, Bouchard sent a demand for immediate surrender, to which the governor replied that they would spill their last blood for king and country. Further he demanded payment for return of the *Santa Rosa.* Next, Bouchard sailed around Point Pinos that evening and disembarked his crew into small boats. Meanwhile the *Santa Rosa,* damaged but not sinking, sat in the bay, neither captured nor destroyed, as the Spaniards conserved their ammunition and lacked the boats and men to secure the vessel. That night, Bouchard stealthily recovered most of the remaining crew from the *Santa Rosa.* The following morning Bouchard's small army, armed with muskets and spears, rowed back into the bay and launched an amphibious frontal assault on *El Castillo*. The Spaniards let loose a volley of fire before spiking their guns and retreating to the *presidio.* The privateers quickly overran the fort, a naked, spear-carrying Sandwich Islander pulling down the red and yellow Spanish flag.

Attention turned to the *presidio* where the Spanish attempted to make a stand. But resistance to superior numbers soon yielded to retreat, as Governor Sola and the remaining *soldados de cuera (*the so-called leather jacketed Spanish soldiers) threw themselves onto their leather-covered wooden saddles and rode off toward Rancho del Rey. In their recounting the battle for Monterey, versions vary. Corney claimed little resistance, and three sailors killed. Officer Jose Maria Piriz said they took the *pueblo* by fire and blood. Governor Sola, in his report to the viceroy, claimed zero casualties among his forces, although he lamented loss of his personal property. Finding only a single drunken settler to take prisoner, the *independistas* began to ransack the town.

According to Corney,

> *"It was well stocked with provisions and goods of every description, which we commenced sending on board the Argentina. The Sandwich Islanders, who were quite naked when they landed, were soon dressed in the Spanish fashion, and all the sailors were employed in searching the houses for money and breaking and ruining every thing."* [9]

Years later, artilleryman Jose Jesus Vallejo would recall that the privateers were no worse than the Spanish, themselves.

By the third day, Governor Sola had been reinforced by soldiers from San Jose and the *presidio* at San Francisco. However, the Spanish troops failed to enter Monterey and counterattack the pirates. Rather, they formed a defensive perimeter to prevent Bouchard from plundering farther inland (which Governor Sola considered something of a victory after his hasty abandonment of the town). Bouchard sent the Governor an ultimatum to exchange the pirate prisoners for the town. Receiving no reply, when the looting was completed, Bouchard ordered the town put to the torch. Anything wooden among the adobe structures was reduced to ashes except for the *presidio* church and the mission at Carmel. Bouchard's war was with the Spanish Crown, not the Church. By the time the soldiers and civilians began to filter back into the still-smoldering Monterey at week's end, the pirate-privateers had repaired the *Santa Rosa,* loaded their limited plunder and sailed away. The people of Monterey began to rebuild. The old *presidio* church is the only construction from before the pirate raid remaining in modern Monterey.

In his report to the viceroy of New Spain, Governor Sola wrote:

> *"After doing the wicked things the rebels do by custom, like relieving their rage by shooting the animals they found, because they could not shoot people, they stole whatever they found useful in the midst of the poverty in which these people live. They left on the 25th at night. But first they set the presidio on fire..."* [10]

Miles away, at Mission Santa Cruz on the north point of the horseshoe-shaped Monterey Bay, the citizens of the *pueblo* at Branciforte heard of the Bouchard raid and feared they would be next. Governor Sola ordered an evacuation and removal of the mission's valuables farther inland. The crew loading the mission stores found the casks of *aguardiente* (a form of brandy) too heavy to take and resorted to consuming them instead. This resulted in some minor damage to the church property, a little pilfering, and some very major hangovers. The privateers never sailed to Santa Cruz.

Before he died in 1883, an elderly former *soldado de cuera* named Jose Maria Amador recounted his memoirs to researcher Thomas Savage. Like his father before him, Amador had been a soldier stationed at the *Presidio* of San Francisco. After retirement, he received a Mexican land grant of Rancho San Ramon, and he was employed by the mission at San Jose. His memoirs were largely forgotten until translated and published in 2005 by Gregorio Mora-Torres, a professor at San Jose State University, in *Californio Voices. The Oral Memoirs of Jose Maria Amador and Lorenzo Asisara. Don* Amador had been part of the reinforcements arriving at Monterey during the Bouchard raid. What follows, with permission of the editor and publisher, is Amador's first-person account of those events:

> *"On November 2, 1818, at two o'clock in the morning, when I was serving as a guard at the Presidio of San Francisco, an urgent message was brought by the soldier Dolores Cantua, with the news that two pirate frigates had entered Monterey, under the command of Hypolite Bouchard. At exactly two o'clock in the*

morning, Lieutenant Gabriel Moraga gathered the troop at the garrison and organized an expedition to Monterey composed of the soldiers that were there and the guards that were picked up as they passed through missions, San Francisco, Santa Clara, and Santa Cruz. The retired soldiers of the town replaced [these guards]. I was chosen to be a part of the expedition. [The expedition] under the command of Don Joe Antonio Sanchez, left during a heavy downpour and reached San Jose when it was getting dark. We took supplies; those who had family got them from their homes; those that did not, brought them. We rode all night and arrived at the King's Ranch [Rancho del Rey] by daybreak. We found Governor Sola in a house of Sergeant Miguel Espinoza who oversaw the ranch. The Governor had dark rings under his eyes that reached down to his sideburns; they were caused by the grief he felt in his soul as a result of Bouchard and his insurgents having forced him and all his men to flee Monterey. Mr. Sola deserved to be called somewhat of a coward. On the following day, in the morning, Captain Luis Arguello arrived with his escort at the government ranch where the governor was staying. He welcomed him with open arms." [11]

Don Amador continues:

"We arrived in Monterey. We found it burning, and the first thing we did was put out the fires. Afterward we went to the fortress. The frigates of Bouchard, which had landed some 350 men, had retreated outside of the bay after sacking and burning the plaza."

"When the frigates entered, we found out they fired off several cannon shots at the presidio; [the volleys] were returned by the bulwark which was under the responsibility of Jose Jesus de Vallejo. He managed to hit three shots of size eight on the side of the black frigate where Bouchard was aboard. During the heat of the battle, Vallejo received an order from Lieutenant

Estudillo to stop fighting. This allowed Bouchard's men to seal the holes of the vessels and leave the bay. Afterwards, the boats came in front of the fortress and unloaded their troops and sailors and proceeded to sack and burn the plaza." [12]

As battles go, it was a small, one-sided affair. Spoils were disappointingly few. Monterey was not wealthy and most everything of value had been removed beforehand. Still, it represented a decisive blow against the Spanish crown and the new pale blue and white flag of Argentina flew above the calm waters of Monterey Bay for a week. It would remain the only seaborn attack on the west coast of North America until a Japanese submarine bombarded oil storage facilities near Santa Barbara in February 1942, following the attack on Pearl Harbor. The exchange between *Santa Rosa* and *el Castillo* remains the only ship-to-shore artillery duel in California history.

Writing in 1891, an early chronicler of these events, William DeWitt Alexander, wrote,

"He [Bouchard] had probably expected to surprise the Spaniards, and to reap a rich booty, and perhaps hoped to gain the people over to the side of the insurgents, and thus to anticipate the revolution, which took place three years later. If so, he failed in both objects. His attack made a deep impression on the imagination of the Californians. As time went on, the story grew. The defenders of Monterey were exalted into heroes and the name of 'that pirate Bouchard' [ese pirata Buchar] inspired terror like that of Captain Kidd on the Atlantic coast [or Drake in the Pacific centuries before]." [13]

A 1964 local newspaper article about the Bouchard raid generated this response from Horacio Baserga, president of the *Circulo Argentino de San Francisco* and a prominent member of the Argentine community in northern California:

"Contrary to what the final results have us believe, Bouchard's intentions in conquering Monterey were not to pillage or destroy the city. His intention was to incite freedom uprisings along the coast as the Argentine

General Don Jose de San Martin and the Venezuelan General Don Simon Bolivar were doing by land." [14]

The politics of Argentine independence were likely unimportant or even unknown to most of the crews onboard *la Argentina and Santa Rosa.* Few of the remaining crew even spoke Spanish. Assembled now from all corners of the globe, these mariners sailed with Bouchard for the chance to plunder and gain riches. Some had been on this voyage for well over a year already and had little to show for it beyond their own survival. Bouchard must have sensed deep frustration himself. He was trying to serve two masters: a new nation fighting for freedom and the desire to return home with enough spoils in the hold of his ships to satisfy his patrons and enhance his own social position. Despite the symbolism of taking Monterey, neither goal had been furthered. He had been informed of a wealthy royalist family and ample plunder at the *pueblo* of Santa Barbara; perhaps there his fortune might change.

Notes:

1. Spanish for *"That Pirate Bouchard!"* Said with scorn.
2. Henry Miller, AZQ quotes.com, https://www.azquotes.com/quotes/1324808. Retrieved September 3, 2022.
3. Elias Castillo, *A Cross of Thorns. The Enslavement of California's Indians by the Spanish Missions,* Fresno, CA: Craven Street Books, 2015, p. 37.
4. Peter Corney, *Voyages in the Northern Pacific. Narrative of Several Trading voyages from 1813 to 1818, Between the Northwest Coast of America, the Hawaiian Islands and China, with Description of the Russian Establishments on the West Coast,* Honolulu, HI: Thos. G. Thrum , Publisher, 1896, p. 44.
5. Ibid.
6. Felipe Fernandez-Armesto, *Our America. A Hispanic History of the United States,* New York: W.W. Norton & Co., 2014, p.118.
7. Barrie Earl Malcolm, *"The Soldiers of Spain's California Army 1769-1821,"* Dissertations and Theses. Paper 4690, M.A. Thesis, Portland State University, 1993, p. 47.
8. Corney, op. cit., p. 121.
9. Ibid., p. 122.
10. *Report of Pablo Vicente de Sola, Governor to the Viceroy of New Spain, Don Juan Ruiz de Apedaca,* December 12, 1818.
11. Jose Maria Amador, Memoirs, *Californio Voices, The Oral Memoirs of Jose Maria Amador and Lorenzo Asisara*, ed. and trans. by Gregorio Mora-Torres, Denton, TX: University of North Texas Press, 2004, p. 71.
12. Ibid, p. 73.

13. William DeWitt Alexander, "Captain Bouchard and the Spanish Pirates," *The Friend,* vol. 49, no. 3, Honolulu, HI, March 1891, p. 19.
14. Horacio Baserga. Letter to the editor, *Monterey Peninsula Herald*, Nov. 7, 1964.

Chapter 8

An Immediate Supply of Powder and Shot

"Old Mission Santa Barbara bears witness to the Franciscan missionary spirit through service to God and God's people, as stewards of the Franciscan heritage in the West, we welcome all and *strive to build a future based on reconciliation and justice which honors all creation and all people."*

–Mission Santa Barbara *mission statement*, 2022

"Yet Serra is revered by many in California as a gentle friar who loved and treated the Indians as if they were his children. In reality, the missions were little more than death camps run by the Franciscan friars where thousands of California's Indians perished."

–Elias Castillo, *A Cross of Thorns*, 2015

Whatever the role Hipolito Bouchard envisioned himself playing as the spark that would ignite rebellion against Spain in Alta California, recent events were saying otherwise. True, he had destroyed a Spanish provincial capital, but realized no political gain from it. He had not captured the governor nor inspired a single person to rise up. The Argentine flag was pulled down in Monterey before *la Argentina* disappeared at sea. The Spanish-born Franciscan friars of the California missions, with their inherent Catholic conservatism, were among the most fervently loyal subjects of the crown. The soldiers at the *presidios* were increasingly indifferent about a regime that often failed to deliver their payroll or supply them with uniforms. shoes and gunpowder, but nevertheless afforded them status, employment and a future stipend in old age. The *mestizo* populations of the *pueblos* and *presidios* were poor, uneducated and apolitical, more concerned about economic matters.

As for the indigenous native population, those who had accepted the Christian faith through belief or fear followed the lead of the mission fathers. The rest of the Native Americans now decades removed from their ancestral lifestyles, had become totally dependent upon the mission environment and the abstract concept of nationality beyond their own tribe could not be imagined.

Such loyalty or ambivalence, however, was not universal throughout the rest of New Spain. The same winds of freedom that had created firestorms of revolution in British America, France, Saint Domingue, and now South America, were also swirling around the plazas and pyramids of Mexico City. Tensions grew between the *peninsulares* who supported both the Spanish crown and the domination of the powerful Catholic church and American-born *criollos, inspired* by the ideas of the Enlightenment. However, royalist support in Mexico was withering, particularly after Spain abrogated its earlier reformed constitution and returned to authoritarian rule. The ever-present wedge issues of race, class, and culture split the people of New Spain.

For over a decade, *criollos* had been agitating for a greater role in the government. The same events in Spain following Napoleon's usurping the Spanish crown that had brought Argentina to the point of open rebellion were slowly galvanizing an independence movement in Mexico as well. These tensions flared into open armed resistance by 1810 with the call for freedom, an end to slavery and land redistribution to the masses by a parish priest named Miguel Hidalgo y Costilla and his protégé Jose Maria Morelos. Although the revolts were suppressed by the ruling power, the struggle endured, marked by sporadic revolts and guerrilla fighting. [1]

Using charts obtained from the Russians and intelligence gleaned at Monterey, Bouchard sailed south in sight of the California coastline before leaving the push of the California current and, taking advantage of prevailing winds, jibed around *Punta de Concepcion,* where the coastline makes a sharp angle to the southeast and he found himself in calmer, warmer water heading toward a seemingly unbroken stretch of sandy beach bordering the shore for miles. A mild rain fell, announcing the coming of what passes for winter in the temperate Mediterranean climate of southern California. The

Sandwich Islanders on board noticed with approval the long, single continuous curl of a perfect surf line.

The ships anchored inside a cove that hid them from observation. A crease in the bluff followed a dry creek up away from the beach. The last of the distinctive monarch butterflies, their rust-colored wings spotted white and yellow, could be seen leaving for their annual migration south toward Mexico. Bouchard and his landing party found a path, clearly well-marked by all the ox-*carreta* tracks, and followed it through the manzanita, scrub oak and wild grasses for a little more than a mile until coming upon a well-tended farm and impressive *hacienda:* Rancho Nuestra Senora del Refugio (Our Lady of Refuge). Hoping to replenish water and resupply his ships, Bouchard approached the house. Rancho Refugio was one of the largest and finest homes in all Alta California. He had come upon the residence of the Ortega family; there was nobody home.

The large, imposing adobe façade of Rancho Refugio faced the sea. It was the jewel of a 26,000-acre tract of land that extended along the coast from Point Conception to the hidden cove at Refugio Bay, about 20 miles from the *presidio* and mission at Santa Barbara. The land grant, more a lease in perpetuity than a title of ownership, was the first of its kind in Alta California during the Spanish era. It was given to Jose Francisco Ortega in 1795 after decades of military service in California. Ortega, a Spaniard originally from Guanajuato, Mexico, had scouted for the original Portola expedition and accompanied Junipero Serra as far as San Francisco Bay. He later served as military commander in both Monterey and Santa Barbara. In retirement, Don Ortega continued to add land to his estate and developed a thriving business breeding horses and raising cattle for the tallow and leather trade. While much of his enterprise was with Spain, Ortega ignored the Spanish prohibition against foreign trade and almost openly traded with ships from other nations. Even the mission fathers would periodically turn a blind eye to the official law and engage in foreign trade through the Ortegas, justifying it by saying sometimes necessity outweighs the law. Ships could load and unload their cargoes in the cove at Refugio Bay without being seen by Spanish customs officials. Even with legal trade, ships would often stash their cargoes on one of the off-shore Channel Islands and bring their nearly empty vessels in to trade with the Spanish, thereby avoiding most of the Spanish duty which could double the cost of the cargo. Then the traders would return to the island, pick up their cargo and return unseen to Refugio Bay and off-load it to the waiting Ortegas duty-free. From the beach, the Ortegas could easily move the contraband to their *rancho,* and then on to the missions at Santa Ynez, Santa Barbara, and as far as Monterey. Russian traders called Don Jose "*Olfama*", from the American reference to Ortega as "the Old Farmer."[2] The Ortegas became one of the wealthiest, most well-known and well-respected families in Alta California.

After the patriarch, Don Jose, had died from a horseback accident in 1798, his family carried on the ranching and smuggling and lavish lifestyle. The family's reputation was so widespread that Bouchard thought he had at last found the treasure he sought. To his dismay, he instead found Rancho Refugio deserted and stripped bare of its contents. Once again, the locals had been forewarned of his arrival and had evacuated as far inland as Mission Santa Ynez, taking most of their possessions with them. Meanwhile, as the privateers searched from building to building, removing any foodstuffs left behind, a squad of mounted soldiers under the command of Sergeant Carlos Antonio Carrillo had been dispatched from the *presidio* at Santa Barbara by Comandante Jose de la Guerra y Noriega, who had previously alerted Governor Sola to Bouchard's approach to Monterey. The troops observed the pirates from the periphery of the *rancho*. After a brief skirmish, greatly outnumbered and thus unwilling to attack the pirates, the cavalry instead sought to capture a prisoner and learn of Bouchard's plans. Three pirates, Lieutenant William Taylor, known on board as "Boston"; Martin Romero of Paraguay; and an African from Guinea, Mateo Jose Pascual, wandered away from their fellow raiders to retrieve an ox-*carreta* to carry their plunder back to the beach. Spanish horse soldiers, among the best light cavalry of their era, swooped in, snared the hapless pirates with their *reatas,* (lariats) *vaquero* (cowboy) style, and dragged the roped crewmen off to jail in Santa Barbara.

According to a family oral history, and years later recounted in the *Gilroy Advocate,* among those who attempted to repel the pirates was John (Jose) Cameron (Gilroy), generally credited with being the first permanent Anglo settler in Alta California. Changing his name to Gilroy, the Scottish sailor had either jumped ship or been discharged for illness in Monterey in 1814 and worked as a cooper for one of Ortega's sons, Ygnacio, on Rancho San Ysidro, near Monterey. After the Bouchard raid there, Gilroy joined reinforcements sent to Santa Barbara – and may have fired the first shot. An 1835 deed from Mexican Governor Castro references Gilroy's personal service against the Chilean invasion.[4] Gilroy later married a granddaughter of Jose Francisco Ortega, and the City of Gilroy adopted his name.

Bouchard waited hours for his missing crew to return before realizing they had been captured. The famous temper, which quite literally could "shiver the timbers" of his crew, roared at being outwitted by the Ortegas and poached of the three crew members by the Spanish troops. In a frenzy, Bouchard ordered all the remaining livestock shot, the throats of the fine horses in the corrals slit, and the entire community burned to the ground. From a distance, observers were appalled at the butchery and feared for their own safety. The raiders filed back down to the beach with their meager booty and the ships sailed out to anchor in one of the many coves at Santa Cruz Island in the Santa Barbara Channel, where Bouchard planned his next move.

The Channel Islands had been one of the most lucrative sources of otter pelts, which turned enormous profits in Hawai'i and Canton. In the hidden harbors of Santa Cruz, traders and smugglers of many nationalities had long found sanctuary, easily evading Spanish import laws which the Spaniards were unable to enforce.[3.] Under a clear sky the following morning, Bouchard took *la Argentina* and *Santa Rosa* through blue water toward Santa Barbara. A mounted patrol followed their progress from the ridge along the beach in sight of the two ships. Acknowledging their presence, the privateers fired a couple of salvos at the shore which fell harmlessly short onto the beach. His approach to Santa Barbara would not be a surprise.

The *pueblo* of Santa Barbara had grown slowly and haphazardly around the *presidio* founded there in 1783 by Fr. Junipero Serra and his accompanying soldiers, seeking a mission site halfway to *Punta Concepcion* along the Channel shoreline. Sometime later, Mission Santa Barbara was begun overlooking the sea and the Goleta Valley. The adobe mission was totally destroyed by a massive earthquake in 1812 and reconstruction of stone was nearly complete by the time of Bouchard's arrival. With its elaborate architectural mix of Spanish and Italianate styles, and immense proportions, the mission would later become known as the "Queen of the Missions." The community numbered about a thousand.

The military commander of Santa Barbara, Jose de la Guerra y Noriega, was known as *"El Capitan."* Born in Spain, he had grown up in Mexico City before being posted to California as a cadet, where he rose quickly through the ranks. De la Guerra served in Monterey before coming to the *presidio* at Santa Barbara, where he assumed command in 1817. Under orders from Governor Sola, de la Guerra oversaw the evacuation of several hundred civilians, including many neophytes, inland to Mission Santa Ynez. The parish priest at Santa Barbara, Fr. Ripoll, armed many other neophytes with bows and arrows and knives, and thirty proficient horsemen were issued lances, the cavalry weapon of choice. With these irregular troops and reinforcements from Monterey, San Luis Obispo and Los Angeles, de la Guerra prepared to defend Santa Barbara.

After Bouchard's ships were pulled into a shallow anchorage, the corsair sent a messenger ashore under a flag of truce. A sailor planted a stake in the sand with a message which demanded return of the three captive crewmen or destruction of the *pueblo.* De la Guerra diplomatically replied that he doubted Governor Sola would approve of the terms, but added that if the pirates wanted a fight, his own soldiers were ready and equal to the challenge. Then he cleverly added that if Bouchard would promise to sail away without further threat to Alta California, he would take responsibility for the prisoner exchange in the name of humanity.

While Bouchard considered the terms from the deck of *la Argentina,* he studied the coastline through his spyglass. What he saw gave him pause. The Spaniards seemed considerably reinforced, taking away any numerical advantage the attackers might have. In fact, de la Guerra had assembled his force and marched them in a continuous loop through a visible *sausal* (a small plantation of willows), changing uniforms with each pass, thus creating the illusion of a much greater fighting force. The bluff succeeded and by afternoon, Bouchard had retrieved his three crewmen. In exchange, he had provided a single hostage, a habitual drunkard named Jose

Molina, who had probably surrendered to Bouchard at Monterey. Furious at the unequal exchange, Governor Sola had Molina arrested for antipatriotic behavior, publicly flogged and imprisoned for a lengthy term. The generous de la Guerra interceded and took Molina into his household staff. After a while, Molina left Santa Barbara and walked the almost 300 dusty miles back to Monterey, where he settled into a corner of a *cantina* and disappeared into the haze of history. The grateful populace of Santa Barbara congratulated de la Guerra for preventing the attack. For Hipolito Bouchard, California was proving a deep disappointment. He had made a promise to leave; but would he keep it?

Before leaving the waters of the Santa Barbara Channel, Bouchard captured a Spanish schooner, *Nuestra Senora de Guadalupe.* Bouchard put aboard a small crew of Sandwich Islanders. But the schooner soon became separated from the frigate *la Argentina.* The Hawaiians intended to return to the Sandwich Islands, but instead sailed north, reaching New Archangel in Alaska, without food or water, in June 1819. The Russians repaired the schooner, renamed it *la Fortuna,* and the seven surviving islanders joined the service of the Russia America Company. The Russians remembered the visit of Bouchard to Fort Ross.

In a letter from Russian Governor Yanoksky to his agent Khlebnikov seeking intelligence, he wrote,

> *"Try to ascertain the condition of California, the progress of the patriots against the royal army in South America, and the allegiance of the schooner (La Fortuna) that came to us...In doing so, however by no means reveal that we know anything about it. Ask about the insurgents' frigates Argentina and Santa Rosa and where they are now."* [5]

By now the Spanish missions farther down the coast were on high alert. Comandante de la Guerra distrusted Bouchard's promise to sail away and sent reinforcements south to thwart further attacks, including two dozen soldiers dispatched to the *presidio* at San Diego. The next closest mission, San Buenaventura, at the opening of the Santa Barbara Channel, was thrown into panic and the padres and their converts evacuated to the sub-mission of Santa Gertrudis

Asistencia, about five miles inland along the Ventura River. As the Argentines sailed past without stopping the following day, prayers of thanks and sighs of relief marked their passing by. The targets of opportunity for plunder were now few and poor. Captain Bouchard decided to pass on Los Angeles *pueblo* as well. Bouchard felt the rewards would not justify the long, hot 20-mile march inland from its port at San Pedro by his increasingly disgruntled crew. Still the constant need to resupply his two ships with water and food for the large crew required landfall somewhere. His options were reduced to San Juan Bay and San Diego. However, he knew that San Diego was well defended by the Castillo de Guijarros on Ballast Point on the mouth of the bay as well as by a reinforced *presidio* now waiting for him. San Juan Bay was known as another harbor for smugglers and offered easy access to the goods stored at nearby Mission San Juan Capistrano. And San Juan Capistrano was not defended by a *presidio.*

As the ships lurked off the southern California coast, the Spanish military was spread thin as it tried to anticipate the pirates' actions. Comandante Francisco Luis Ruiz of San Diego split his forces and sent some thirty soldiers under Alferez Don Santiago Arguello to San Juan Capistrano and a detachment was ordered from Los Angeles as well. Meanwhile, life went on as normal at the bustling San Juan community of about a thousand people. Though they had been warned weeks earlier about the possible pirate threat and had been ordered by the governor to prepare to evacuate, the two padres, Jose Barona and Geronimo Boscana, were disdainful of being intimidated by mere pirates. The plan called for evacuation to San Antonio de Pala, a sub-mission of Mission San Luis Rey at "the first tidings of Visart's [Bouchard's] arrival." But that was fifty miles away. The padres opted instead to take the mission property and civilians to an adobe mission station used by *vaqueros* eight miles away on Trabuco Creek. Only when a lookout spotted *la Argentina* and *Santa Rosa* entering San Juan Bay on December 15, did the padres begin a hasty retreat to Trabuco Rancho, with the local Indian neophytes carrying whatever they could. When soldiers checked on the mission that day, they found only a 72-year-old retired sergeant named Jose Antonio Yorba left behind with a handful of servants. The mission was locked and the *pueblo* was abandoned.[6]

Late afternoon shadows fell across the water as the ships rounded what would be later known as Dana Point into San Juan Capistrano Bay.

According to Peter Corney onboard Santa Rosa,

> *"We again ran into a snug bay...where we anchored under a flag of truce. The bay is well sheltered, with a most beautiful town and mission, about two leagues from the beach. The Commodore sent his boat on shore, to say if they would give us an immediate supply of provisions, we would spare their town."* [7]

Bouchard demanded a response within half an hour.

Ensign Arguello knew he was outnumbered ten-to-one and the arrival of de la Guerra with reinforcements was unsure. The mission padres had even failed to arm the neophytes with bows and arrows. He had no time to refer the demand to his superiors. Rather he told the launch crew they were welcome to land, and they would receive "an immediate supply of powder and shot." Bouchard saw Arguello's bluff for the empty threat it was and took it as a personal insult.

According to Corney,

> *"The Commodore was very much incensed at this answer and assembled all the officers to know what was to be done...It was, therefore, agreed to land, and give it up to be pillaged and sacked."* [8]

By dawn the following day Spanish reinforcements had arrived as Peter Corney led a raiding party of 140 men ashore on the morning tide. While the pirates assembled on the beach, mounted Spanish cavalry feigned a charge, let loose a volley of shots and quickly retreated to protect the road away through Trabuco Canyon. The sailors quickly occupied the town and began plundering wildly, fueled by large quantities of wine and aguardiente found in the cellars of the mission complex. Wanton destruction was accompanied by the steady peel of the mission bells as the drunken sailors ignored the sanctity of the mission chapel and, searching for treasure, clambered over the rubble of the unrestored great stone church, destroyed by earthquake in

1812. As discipline broke down completely, Corney ordered the men to gather up the spoils and prepare to return to the ships. Many sailors were too drunk to stand let alone haul heavy objects nearly two miles to the beach. The most inebriated were lashed to the field guns and dragged back down the path; many others dropped or threw away their prizes along the way. Many of the buildings – again excepting the church – were put to the torch.

Back onboard his frigate, Bouchard surveyed the sorry state of his crew and ordered them to their hammocks to sleep off the drink. The following day two score of the worst offenders were subjected to the lash, as the Frenchman punished his disorderly crew for their behavior and failure to retrieve most of the plunder. On taking report, he learned that four sailors were missing and presumed captive. Knowing the enemy to have now been significantly reinforced and apprised that the four crew were possibly deserters, Bouchard, disgusted by the entire affair, decided to cut his losses, avoid further contact with the soldiers and sail away, leaving the four crewmen ashore to their fate. In fact, the four sailors, Pedro Saldivar, Nicholas Echevarria, a young Scottish drummer named John Rose and Mateo Jose Pasqual (the same sailor captured earlier at Refugio) had hidden in a building during the melee and surrendered themselves to the Spanish. Governor Sola determined they had been onboard the privateers against their will and were ready to submit to Catholicism and Spanish sovereignty and allowed them to remain in California.

San Juan Capistrano was still smoldering as Father Borona, Father Boscana, the soldiers and Indians returned to survey the destruction. Only adobe walls remained; wood construction and the Indian huts of branches and reeds were totally gone. Months later, the padres would blame the military for not adequately protecting the mission, which Ensign Arguello rebutted in a letter to Governor Sola. But every member of the community was alive, all the religious objects of the mission had been safely spirited away beforehand, and much of the plunder retrieved from the littered pathway.

Don Antonio Ignacio Avila, *a juez de campo* (municipal or camp judge) in Los Angeles, was among the reinforcements sent to San Juan Capistrano. Years later, his son, Don Juan Avila, told researchers from the Bancroft Library at University of California at Berkley about his father's recollections of the incident:

> *"Bouchard was anchored at Boca de la Playa. My father placed himself at the disposal of Ensign Santiago Arguello. Arguello, instead of awaiting the enemy to fall upon them as soon as he saw them disembark and advance on the mission, took flight with his entire command to situate himself out of danger on the high hill to the east." Avila protested that the Spaniards should attack but Arguello refused, citing liability for any damages incurred to mission property. "Finally, the insurgents embarked, almost all of them intoxicated but Arguello would let no one approach the beach until the ships had disappeared. In San Juan Capistrano, the fathers had taken to the Tuburco rancho the greater portion of the valuables which they had in the mission. They only left the wine, brandy and olive oil and large quantity of seed. The first three articles were spilled about by the insurgents who opened the pipes and pressed their lips against the holes and thus became intoxicated to the extent that in their withdrawal they no longer went in formation and it may have been an easy matter to make prisoners of them."* [9]

No longer believing Bouchard's promise not to attack, de la Guerra returned to Santa Barbara and Arguello and Carrillo took their troops to defend San Diego, the anticipated next target. For the Spanish in Alta California, the Bouchard raids had destroyed some property and shattered some nerves, but no lives had been lost and no revolutionary activity has been fomented. Governor Sola's strategy of mass evacuations and removal of anything of value had proved successful. The raids did, however, show other interested nations that California was vulnerable, and the Spanish ultimately were unable to defend it properly. For the privateers, Alta California had proved a bust. No ships, no spoils, no effect on independence. They had lost crew to cannon, capture and desertion. It was time to sail another sea.

Notes:

1. By 1821, three years after the exploits of Hipolito Bouchard, Mexico finally achieved full independence from Spain. Interestingly, the administration of Alta California seemed to slide seamlessly into acceptance of the new regime. However, Mexico was even less equipped to support this far-off province. The missions slowly slipped into decline and were eventually secularized in 1834. The vast mission lands were distributed, and the era of the great Mexican *ranchos* was ushered in, lasting until United States annexation of California and the Treaty of Guadalupe Hidalgo in 1848.

2. Susan L. Morris, Glenn J. Farris, Steven J. Schwartz, Irina Vladi, L. Wender and Boris Dralyuk, "Murder, Massacre and Mayhem on the California Coast, 1814-1815: Newly Translated Russian American Company Documents Reveal Company Concern Over Violent Clashes," *Journal of California and Great Basin Anthropology,* vol. 34, no. 1, 2014, p. 98, https://www.nps.gov.>subjects>upload>JCGBA, retrieved July 7, 2022.

3. Edward Selden Spaulding, A Brief Story of Santa Barbara, The Santa Barbara Historical Society, Pacific. Coast Publishing Co., 1964, pp. 31-32.

4. *Book B of Deeds,* p. 65, 18 October 1835, reported in *Gilroy Advocate*, July 31, 1869.

5. "*Secret Instructions from Governor Yanovsky to Agent Khlebnikov about a Voyage to Alta California in the Brig Il'mena.*" 1 No.11. New Archangel, 31 May 1820, in James R. Gibson and Alexei A. Istomin, with Valery A. Tishkov, Russian California 1806-1860. A History in Documents, vol 1, London: Hakluyt Society, 2014.

6. Eric Plunkett, "The Saga of Orange County's 'Pirates'" – *San Juan Capistrano Visitor Series Part 8, Visions of California,* blogpost, *October 28, 2018,* https://www.visions of Californiablogspot.com>2018, retrieved Sept. 10, 2022.

7. Peter Corney, Voyages in the Northern Pacific, Honolulu, HI: Thomas G. Thrum, Publishers, 1869, p. 124.

8. Ibid.

9. Jan Siegel, "Don Juan Avila Recounts the Pillaging of Capistrano," *Capistrano Dispatch,* April 13-26, 2012.

Chapter 9
False Flags

"They are a voice of the past
Of an age that is fading fast
Of a power austere and grand,
When the flag of Spain unfurled
Its folds o'er this western world
And the Priest was lord of the land."

–Henry Wadsworth Longfellow,
The Bells of San Blas (1882) [1]

Captain Bouchard's mood darkened like the sky as he raced south ahead of one of the early northern Pacific winter storms. He was anxious to put California waters astern, as well as out of memory. Perhaps southern latitudes would be more welcoming for a privateer in search of Spanish ships to plunder. Three hundred miles south of San Diego, they put into Sebastian Vizcaino Bay, on the arid coast of Baja (lower) California. There the Christian crewmen of *la Argentina* and *Santa Rosa* would celebrate the Christmas holiday of 1818 on the Isla de Cedros.

Isla de Cedros, the largest of this Mexican island group, was an early homeland of aboriginal Americans. In fact, many archeologists would later find evidence there that earliest Americans may have first migrated through the north and south continents by sea rather than land. The natives called the island *Huamalegua,* or "Island of Fogs" before the Spanish explorer Francisco de Ulloa mistook the local pine trees for cedars and dubbed it Isla de Cedros in 1539. For decades the island had been a source of freshwater and game for Dutch, English and other nationality pirates preying upon the Manila galleons along the Mexican coast. More recently it had attracted seal and sea otter hunters, particularly Russians.

On the west side of the island heavy surf pounded the rocky shore and the island was open to battering by Pacific hurricanes. Instead, the ships anchored on the south-east side near a make-shift village of Russian fur trapper huts. A handful of Russians had been landed on the island by an American brig. Together with the sailors, they made daily hunting forays for the deer and feral goats that lived among the live oak, juniper and Monterey pines of the higher elevations. The sailors fished for the plentiful yellowtail and amberjack and learned to enjoy sea lion and elephant seal hearts and tongues. While the ships were being refitted, half a dozen of the crew stole a whaleboat and deserted in heavy fog. Enraged, Bouchard sent boats in pursuit, but after three days the search parties returned without the deserters. Bouchard vowed their death, but resigned to leave without them, further depleting his crew.

By mid-January, now in the new calendar year of 1819, Bouchard sailed past the arches that marked the tip of the Baja California peninsula at Cabo San Lucas. On the 24th, the privateers captured and scuttled the merchant ship *Las Animas* , keeping its cargo of Nicaraguan cacao before heading for the Mexican coastal port of San Blas, in the present state of Nayarit. Dropping anchor in the lee of Isla Maria Madre in the Tres Marias archipelago off the Nayarit coast, the Argentines foraged for food and while digging for fresh water, found ore that may have been deposits of silver. The islands, named for three Biblical women named Mary by explorer Diego Hurtado de Mendoza, a cousin of conquistador Hernan Cortez, were heavily wooded and offered abundant small game, fish, rays, sharks and turtles.

According to Peter Corney,

> *"We found a root resembling tarrow [sic., taro] of the Sandwich Islands; the Islanders cooked some of it in the island fashion, and immediately after they had eaten of it their bodies and faces became swelled and bloated in a terrible manner, some died in a few days, and others lingered for ten days in the greatest agony. The Commodore lost twelve men in this manner."* [2]

After several weeks, with his crew even further depleted, Bouchard sailed to the mainland to initiate a blockade of San Blas harbor, hoping to trap a treasure galleon inside.

Enroute, the privateers encountered the British ship *Good Hope,* of the Calcutta Company, out from Bengal to Mazatlán, detaining it for several days and relieving it of Spanish merchandise and various papers. Bouchard interrogated Captain Silvester Ramsay about developments in South America. Ramsay confirmed rumors about the progress of San Martin in liberating Chile and the early stages of the offensive in Peru. This was the first real communication Bouchard had received in almost twenty months at sea. Bouchard completed a tersely written report and messages to the Director Pueyrredon and his patron Vicente Echeverria in Buenos Aires, as well as to Chilean leader Bernardo O'Higgins and Jose de San Martin, offering his ships in their service. He entrusted this communication in the care of Captain Ramsay, who was allowed to sail for Chile. When Echevarria received the news, he realized he would have little gain from Bouchard's long voyage. Nevertheless, he made the captain's news public and the local citizenry proclaimed Bouchard a hero. Norberta Bouchard now hoped for her husband's imminent return to support the family.[3]

Established in 1768 by the Spanish Visitor General Jose de Galvez as a military port, San Blas had become one of the busiest harbors and shipyards of the Pacific Americas, serving the Manila galleons until eclipsed by Acapulco and Mazatlán. After 1810, San Blas opened to trade, using Mexican silver to pay for imported goods that had been traded in Panama. San Blas was also the home port to the annual supply ships for Alta California and for Spanish expeditions into the Pacific northwest to contest the Russians and Americans. Over time, the shallow harbor had silted up and the oppressive climate made San Blas less attractive.

Bouchard spent the month of February at anchor off San Blas or sailing back and forth, effectively closing the port, though no prizes were to be had. At one point a brig-schooner appeared under the Spanish flag and the ships exchanged a harmless volley of cannon fire, before it sailed away with l*a Argentina* and *Santa Rosa* in pursuit. The quicker stranger eluded the frigate and slipped away to sea. In fact, it had been a Chilean privateer, *El Chileno,* flying the Spanish flag in a false flag tactic often employed by Bouchard as well. Bouchard waited two days for this ship to reappear before abandoning the blockade of San Blas and searching out Acapulco. It would not be the only time these ships would encounter each other in confusion, illegally flying the false flag of an enemy nation. A reconnaissance boat slipped into Acapulco harbor and returned to report no significant vessels there. Some historians have speculated that this was the scene of a clandestine meeting between Bouchard and the Mexican revolutionary hero Vicente Guerrero. After Lieutenant Tomas Espora and the ship's doctor made an unsuccessful foray to obtain fresh food along the beaches at Camamas, Bouchard sailed on.

If, as playwright Tennessee Williams said, "Mexico is the front door to South America,"[4] then Central America is the long foyer. The narrow land bridge that connects two great American continents today comprises the five nations of Costa Rica, El Salvador, Guatemala, Honduras and Nicaragua. But from the 16th century *Conquista* (conquest) until independence in 1821, Central America was part of the Viceroyalty of New Spain and administered by the captain general of Guatemala in Antigua and later Guatemala City. The skinny isthmus of Panama, in the far south, connected Central America to the Viceroyalty of New Granada (Colombia). The Spanish conquest effectively wiped out the advanced civilizations that had populated the humid, swampy lowlands and fertile mountain regions, which had thrived in Central America for centuries. The indigenous called it "the time of darkness and toil." During the first decades of the 19th century, independence movements flared and sputtered in El Salvador and elsewhere as Central American *criollos* reacted to events in Spain. When Mexico finally declared independence in 1821, it recognized Central America's right to self-determination. The Congress of Central America declared absolute independence in 1823, but the united region soon dissolved into civil war and splintered into separate nations.[5] (Much of Central America would become economic colonies of the United States. The area gained strategic importance with completion of the Panama Canal in 1914.)

Many observers have noted the similarity between several Central American national flags and the broad blue and white bands of the Argentine flag, first brought to Central America by Hipolito Bouchard.

At the port of Sonsonate, where almost eighty inches of annual rain and the rich volcanic soils had created a thriving trade for the bounty of the cacao plantations, Bouchard 's fortunes rebounded. An advance scouting party reported fat brigs bobbing in the harbor at the mouth of the River of Many Waters (or 400 waters) in the native Nahautal language. Outside the harbor, *la Argentina* took another brig captive without resistance after ordering no quarter given. Encouraged at brighter prospects he moved on, prize in hand.

On April 2nd he approached the well protected port of Realejo on the Nicaraguan coast, which for centuries had been one of the most thriving shipbuilding and commercial centers of the Spanish Empire. Originally established to support Pedro de Alvarado's invasion of Peru, once the ships' pilots mastered the turbulent currents and strong offshore *papagayos* (winds), blowing up from the Nicoya Peninsula of Costa Rica, Realejo's abundant supply of upland pine and hardwood and indigenous labor, brought prosperity to the port. African slaves were imported to supplement the native Nicaraguans in the production of cotton and fibers used in the important manufacture of rope. Consequently, Realejo had always been a target for pirates. Although Francis Drake had sailed past Realejo, John Davis sacked Granada and Leon upriver before plundering Realejo in 1665, Edward Davis plundered in 1685 and was followed by the French buccaneer Francois Grogniet. However, by the 18th century, competition from shipbuilders in Manila, depletion of resources and the silting up of the mangrove-lined estuary sent Realejo into decline. By Bouchard's visit, it had been replaced by Sonsonate as the major port in Central America. [6]

The captain deemed 60 crew sufficient to take a pair of armed longboats ashore for an assault under his personal command. As the privateers rowed into the estuary, they encountered four ships at anchor, effectively blocking entrance to the port. The port watch sounded the alarm and Spanish soldiers, reinforced by some 200 militia from Guatemala, mounted a stiff defense. Instead, Bouchard directed *la Argentina* and *Santa Rosa* to approach and engage the four ships. The cannonade was fierce as the two privateers in turn crossed the bows of the anchored ships and delivered broadsides of shot and cannister. Unable to maneuver at anchor and side to side, the Spanish ships finally called for quarter. Before the Argentines could board one of the ships, a score of Spanish sailors jumped overboard, rather than be taken prisoner. Bouchard ignored their cries. When the owners of the brig *San Antonio* (also called *la Concordia)* and the goleta (schooner) *Lauretana* offered a combined ransom of only ten thousand pesos, Bouchard had the two ships burned to the waterline and sunk in the harbor. He kept the remaining ships, a lugger named *San Jose* or *Neptuno* and a schooner *Maria Sophia,* which he immediately dispatched to Buenos Aires.

Infantry Officer Piriz recorded the event:

> *"Ten thousand pesos they offered but since that was not our objective without debilitating their Navy, we burned them beforehand transferring to the other two all their artillery, supplies and prisoners, which we took with us."* [7]

Commodore Bouchard directed the organization of his newly enlarged fleet from onboard the *Santa Rosa de Chacabucco.* Meanwhile *la Argentina* sighted a merchant frigate called *la Cazadora* and set off in pursuit. Suddenly a third ship appeared, the corsair *El Chileno,* which previously had sparred with the Argentines off San Blas, once again flying the Spanish flag in deception. As the stranger bore down on the *Santa Rosa,* Bouchard turned to meet it forcefully, despite having a crew of mostly inexperienced Sandwich Island gunners and few guns. The Chilean volley killed three Argentines and wounded several, as well as damaging the rigging and hull *of Santa Rosa.* As the Chileans readied their grappling hooks for boarding, they struck the Spanish flag and raised that of Chile. Stupefied that he was engaged with an ally, Bouchard raised the Argentine ensign and the fighting stopped immediately. As both ships had deployed false flags, they were equally to blame for the affair. Bouchard petitioned Captain Coll of *el Chileno* for use of his surgeon to treat the wounded and asked the Chilean ship to carry letters to Valparaiso for him. Instead, Coll saluted Bouchard as a comrade in arms, and sailed away to find *la Cazadora,* which had slipped away in the smoke and confusion of battle.

On the 3rd of April, after 21 months of a globe-spanning voyage, the patriot in Bouchard trumped the privateer and he committed himself to return to South America in the service of liberation. Realejo had been his greatest success of the long adventure. He had now doubled his fleet and their holds contained at least a modest amount of plunder. But his ships were battered and his remaining crew – he had buried scores at sea – were exhausted. He consulted his charts to plot a course through equatorial waters to the friendly embrace of Valparaiso, Chile, and eventually back to Buenos Aires. Valparaiso was still three months before the wind into the future and his arrival below the equator would turn his world upside down.

Notes:

1. First verse of Wadsworth's last poem, inspired by an article "Typical Journeys and Country Life in Mexico," by William Henry Bishop, Harper's Magazine, March 1882. Wasdsworth never visited San Blas.
2. Peter Corney, Voyages in the Northern Pacific, Honolulu, H.I.: Thos. G. Thrum, Publisher, 1896, p. 126.
3. Miguel Angel De Marco, Bouchard: Halcon de los Mares. Corsario de la Libertad, Buenos Aires: Emece, 2018, p. 196.
4. Tennessee Williams, The Night of the Iguana, New Directions Publishing, 2009, p. 11.
5. "Mexican and Central American Independence: A Historic Backdrop for Present Challenges," teleSUR, https://www.telesurenglish.net>analysis, retrieved Sept. 22, 2022.
6. David R. Rodell and James J. Parson, "Realejo: A Forgotten Colonial Port and Shipbuilding Center in Nicaragua, Hispanic American Historical Review, Duke University Press, May 1, 1971, https://www.read.dukepress.edu>hahr>articlerealejo:forgottencolonialportands hipbuildingcenterinnicaragua, retrieved Oct. 1, 2022.
7. Jose Maria Piriz, in Miguel Angel DeMarco, op. cit. p. 199.

Chapter 10
Admirals and Liberators

O'er the glad waters of the dark blue sea
Our thoughts as boundless, and our souls as free
Far as the breeze can bear, the billows foam
Survey our empire and behold our home!

–George Gordon, Lord Byron,
Canto I, *The Corsair* (1814)

On a dreary, mid-winter July afternoon in 1819, Lord Thomas Cochrane sat at his desk in his comfortable lodgings not far from the waterfront of Valparaiso, Chile, trying to catch up with his correspondence. He sighed as he once again wrote to Supreme Director of Chile Bernardo O'Higgins, imploring – no, demanding – that he be provided more money and men for the Chilean navy. Cochrane was vice admiral of the newly formed navy, 10th Earl of Dundonald in Britain, and simply the most famous, feared and admired naval hero in the world, since the death of Horatio Nelson at Trafalgar. Somewhere buried in the pile of paperwork on his desktop was a report of indictment for piracy for a recently arrived privateer sailing for the United Provinces, Chile's ally, who had been arrested upon arriving in port on July 13th. The captain-privateer under arrest was named Hipolito Bouchard. It was not the first time Bouchard had been Cochrane's prisoner.

Almost twenty years earlier, Cochrane had taken the captured French warship *Genereux* and all its crew to the British-held island of Minorca, after the failed French relief effort of Malta. Among the French prisoners had been a young gunnery sailor, then known as Andre-Paul Bouchard. Of course, there was no reason for Cochrane to have remembered Bouchard by any name. Cochrane's own career had been stunning in his achievements. Rising quickly through the ranks of the British navy, Cochrane adhered to Nelson's admonition to "Never mind maneuvers. Always go after them." Often contemptuous and defiant of authority, Cochrane was nevertheless the most gallant, clever and deceptive officer in the British fleet during the French Revolutionary and the Napoleonic wars. In one year alone he had captured or destroyed 53 French warships. Napoleon, himself, called Cochrane *le loup des mers* (the Sea Wolf). The Spanish knew him as *El Diablo* (the Devil). Following the Napoleonic campaigns, Cochrane stood successfully for parliament as a radical Whig. Although popular with his constituents, Cochrane proved difficult with his fellow parliamentarians as well as the British Admiralty. In 1814, he had been implicated in the Great Stock Exchange Fraud, which spread unfounded rumors of Napoleon's death. Cochrane was convicted and sentenced to a year's imprisonment, a fine and time in the public pillory (the public humiliation was later dismissed). He was summarily cashiered from the navy, expelled from parliament and stripped of his knighthood and naval honors. Making himself available in the marketplace for experienced naval officers, he was approached by emissaries of San Martin and O'Higgins, and accepted the command of the Chilean navy in formation.

Two full years after setting out from Buenos Aires, *la Argentina* returned to a South American port at Valparaiso, preceded by *Santa Rosa de Chacabuco, Maria Sophie* and *Neptune.*

Peter Corney wrote,

> *"On the 9th of July we made the harbour [sic] of Valparaiso. His Majesty's ships Andromache and Icarus were here, with all Lord Cochrane's squadron fitting out for Lima. On the 17th, the Argentina arrived in very great distress for provisions and water; she had buried about forty men; the ships were laid up and most of the crews entered on board the Chilean fleet."* [1]

What Corney fails to report is that when he arrived in port ahead of Bouchard, he was unable to adequately explain to port authorities who they were or on whose behalf they sailed. At first this was due to a difference in languages spoken, but it was more the fog of suspicion that hovered over Valparaiso, on constant alert for royalist insurgents and Spanish spies. Corney's invalid ship's papers and letter of marque had been handwritten by a certain captain Bouchard, not the government in Buenos Aires. Evidence that the *Maria Sophie* might be a Danish ship added to the confusion. Rumors of an attack upon a British ship in Indonesian waters, brought demands from the British naval attaché for an investigation. Corney and the crew members were detained under guard and the ships impounded. The Chilean government was very cautious about avoiding international incidents that could compromise the legitimacy of the new nation.

Lord Cochrane wrote to the Ministry of the Navy,

> *"All the antecedents concerning these ships confirm the opinion that I had formed from the beginning that they are pirates. Nothing can better contribute to placing the Chilean navy on a respectable footing before the European nations than a solemn process and a presentation of those punishable procedures, such as the condemnation of those ships for the use of the state [as pirates]."* [2]

As a result, as Bouchard entered the harbor, expecting a friendly welcome, he learned his other ships had been seized and he, himself, was to be accused of piracy. Confused and infuriated, Bouchard demanded adjudication by an Argentine court, and he resisted arrest, calling for his skeleton crew to fix bayonets. Bouchard's officer staff defused the confrontation, and the captain was removed in custody to the Chilean ship *San Martin.* Anger and humiliation, punctuated by bouts of despair, accompanied the Frenchman as he awaited trial in Santiago.

In jail, Hipolito Bouchard lamented,

> *"I am imprisoned here. I have done more or less the same as Columbus. Columbus discovered America and ended up in prison. And I have traveled around the world holding the Argentine flag and I am living a similar destination."* [3]

Through his depression, the almost arrogant self-regard of the man comes across as he equates to Columbus.

The legal proceedings against Hipolito Bouchard lasted more than four months. Charges of various violations of the rules of privateering were thrown against him, as well as complaints against his personal cruelty and brutal behavior, brought by several resentful crew members. Some saw the entire procedure as a veiled effort by the Chilean navy – or by Cochrane himself – to appropriate the four ships and cargoes for their cash values to augment the Chilean fleet readying for the invasion of Peru. Others viewed it as a power struggle between two adolescent nations and a domineering Great Britain. Most observers felt sympathetic toward the master mariner who had sailed around the Pacific, seizing dozens of enemy ships in furious land and sea battles, only to be subjected to abuse by a seemingly ungrateful independence movement at home. Argentines, in particular, took umbrage that their flag had sailed the world for the first time with Bouchard and was now being disrespected.

Mid-way through the trial, Lord Cochrane sailed from Valparaiso to begin the siege of Callao and Lima. Earlier that year, Cochrane had assumed command of the frigate *O'Higgins* and initiated a blockade of ports along the Peruvian coast. Unsuccessful at taking the Real Felipe fortress at Callao, he turned his attention to the heavily fortified stronghold of Valdivia, inside the Coral Bay at the mouth of the Mapuche River, protected by a string of seven forts. In a daring nighttime move involving only two ships and some 300 men, Cochrane launched an amphibious assault, capturing all the forts and sacking the city. The Spanish fled to the Chiloe Archipelago, their last remaining foothold in Chile. Cochrane was lionized by Chilenos. Although they often disagreed, Cochrane, Jose de San Martin and Bernardo O'Higgins concurred that Chilean security remained at risk as long as the Spanish maintained their strong presence in Peru. Cochrane next was ordered to convoy San Martin's Liberation Army for the assault on Peru.

In addition to his naval brilliance and audacity, there was another facet to Lord Cochrane. He was deeply suspicious and resentful of authority. He believed the governmental powers were jealous of his fame and accomplishments and in conspiracy to withhold the full support he needed. Cochrane complained bitterly and often.

In his memoirs, he wrote of his victory at Valdivia:

> *"The annexation of this province [Valdivia], at one blow conferred on Chili complete independence, averting the contemplated necessity for fitting out a powerful military expedition for the attainment of that object, vitally essential to her very existence as an independent state."*

But he then continued,

> *"Notwithstanding these advantages, not a penny in the shape of reward, either for this or any previous service was paid to myself, the officers, or seamen, nevertheless the Government appropriated the money [from the sale of captured ships and stores]...."*

More than once, Cochrane threatened to resign his position and he declined the offer of an estate from the liberated territory. He wrote, *"Seeing that I was determined not to be trifled with and shamed by my offer of applying the estate to the payment of my men,"* General San Martin was prompted to intervene and secured payment for the sailors and assured Cochrane of receiving what was owed him, at which point Cochrane accepted the grant of the estate and the government's I.O.U. of some 67,000 pesos. This episode clearly illustrates Cochrane's prowess as a negotiator but also as a true mercenary. As a soldier of fortune, he had sold his skills in return for financial reward, not for idealism. Indeed, upon accepting the Chilean commission, Cochrane had reportedly claimed he would reap more honors and wealth from the venture than anyone since the Duke of Wellington, having defeated Napoleon at Waterloo. San Martin criticized Cochrane's interest in financial gain and dubbed him *"El Metalico Lord* (The Metalic Lord)." [4]

The one person whose authority outweighed Cochrane, General Jose de San Martin, was indisposed on the other side of the Andes and unable to provide any defense for Bouchard. Bouchard did, however, have defenders. Ships' officers, including Tomas Espora testified that no neutral country ships had been harassed. Argentine representative Tomas Guido argued that any ships attacked had lacked the proper patents and registration papers, as required by maritime law. As for the *Maria Sophie,* she was indeed originally Danish, but had been captured and in the service of Spain for months and was therefore fair prey by the Argentines. In October 1819, the court upheld the argument that Bouchard's actions were authorized by the government of United Provinces and were clearly that of a privateer, not a pirate. The issue of ships flying a false flag became a red herring despite the practice being clearly considered piratical by Article 24 of the *Provisional Regulation for Corso.* Ironically, Lord Cochrane, himself, had famously used the deceit more than once in his sea battles with the French and Spanish.

Ultimately the outcome hinged on the expiration of the original letter of marque. Stretching the truth, Bouchard argued that earlier in his cruise he had been directed to seek out and detain the *Santa Rosa de Chacabuco,* which crew had mutinied and gone rogue. It is unlikely he ever received such orders in the middle of the Indian Ocean or anywhere else. Buenos Aires had not known where Bouchard was and there is no paper trail. He likely saw *Santa Rosa* for the first time at Hawai'i, where he forged such orders for the benefit of the Hawaiian king. Bouchard claimed that search justified adding an additional seven-month extension to his letter of marque. Regardless of whether this defense found traction with the court, the issue was redirected to Argentine authorities. Before the court handed down its verdict a detachment of Argentine soldiers stationed in Valparaiso liberated the impounded frigate and raised the blue and white flag of Argentina in a show of support for the commodore. Bouchard was acquitted on December 9th. The decision read: "He is acquitted of the instant trial and its formalities. Set free and return the Argentine frigate and other ships taken in his privateering."[5]

At this point, Peter Corney, loyal second in command of the privateers and architect in Hawai'i of the invasion of Alta California, decided on a change of course. As he wrote in his memoir of his time aboard the *Santa Rosa,*

> *"I now applied to Captain Bouchard for my pay and prize money, and told him I was heartily sick of the service of the independents, and that I intended to go to England in the first vessel that sailed for that country, the port being then embargoed on account of the*

> *expedition going against Peru; he replied that he could not pay me, unless I continued in the service and took the ship to Buenos Ayres; which I declined doing"* [6]

Corney bitterly concludes,

> *"We do not find sufficient interest in the sequel of these adventures to render it advisable to give the details, and shall only add, that the writer of this journal, Mr. Corney, arrived in London on the 15th of February 1820, and after an absence of nearly seven years, full of vicissitudes."* [7]

Hipolito found himself a free man. But with the defection of Corney and his former crew dispersed into the Chilean navy or elsewhere, he also found himself alone. Reclaiming his ships, he discovered their cargoes had been appropriated by the Chilean government and the ships, themselves, cannibalized by the navy, guns and rigging and even some wooden planking removed to outfit other ships. Without any source of income, Bouchard leased out the schooner *Neptune* to haul 80 tons of clay for cannon molds back to Buenos Aires. On board as ships officers were his two brothers-in-law, the Merlo siblings, who had endured and survived the entire two-year voyage and would act as Bouchard's emissaries in Buenos Aires, explaining his dire financial straits and his intentions to return to Buenos Aires within the coming days. This was disingenuous; Bouchard had already decided to cast his fortune with the continued efforts for South American liberty.

After learning the bitter lesson about the expiration date on his letter of marque. Bouchard petitioned patron Don Vicente Echevarria for new letters for the four ships. After Echevarria persuaded the new United Provinces supreme director Jose Rondeau, by naming a small vessel after him, the new letters arrived, good for only eight months. Bouchard next sent the *Maria Sophie on* to Buenos Aires. Echevarria would realize less than ten percent of his initial investment from the sale of *Maria Sophie* and *Neptune*; his patience with Bouchard was growing thin. With limited time, few resources and fewer options, Bouchard fell back on what he knew best. He would go back to sea.

Bouchard's two remaining vessels, *la Argentina* and *Santa Rosa de Chacabuco* were both badly battered and no longer outfitted as ships of war. However, they were still seaworthy. In another humiliation for the proud Frenchman, he offered his ships in the service of the Liberation Expedition of Peru – not as privateers but as cargo ships and troop transports. As if to save the reputation of his flagship, Bouchard retired the name *la Argentina,* reclaiming her original name *Consecuencia.* On board was a regiment of *granaderos,* including now battle-hardened veterans of Bouchard's old cavalry unit. Even more degrading, the *Santa Rosa* now ferried cattle and other military supplies. But the transactional arrangement gave Bouchard an income, a pathway out of debt and a future. He would tolerate being under the command of Cochrane; he would follow San Martin to the ends of the earth.

The combined Chilean-Argentine expeditionary force sailed from Valparaiso on August 20th under the shared command of San Martin and Lord Cochrane. Fourteen transports, including *Consecuencia* and *Santa Rosa,* were escorted by eight warships. The strategy was to encircle Lima from the interior with San Martin's army and for the navy to form a semicircle at sea effectively sealing off Callao and Lima. Before leaving Valparaiso, San Martin exhorted his troops that it was a campaign of liberation, not conquest. Aware that royalist forces in Peru, reinforced by veteran soldiers from Spain, remained very strong, San Martin advocated a war of propaganda, hoping to convince the Peruvians to rise up and seek independence. Along with his artillery, San Martin's army marched with a printing press, distributing messages of liberty throughout the countryside in an early form of psychological warfare. Cochrane, the more aggressive of the two commanders, urged quicker, stronger offensive effort. In a running dialogue with the Viceroy of Peru, Jose de la Serna, San Martin urged acceptance of a constitutional monarchy in order to avoid war, but he was rebuffed. Instead, de la Serna advocated accepting the liberalized Spanish Constitution of 1812, which San Martin rejected. When diplomacy failed, successive military reversals in the highlands forced de la Serna to abandon Lima and the liberators were able to occupy the city by mid-July 1821. San Martin declared Peruvian independence on July 28 with himself named Protector of the new state. It is quite possible Bouchard was in the capital to witness events.

Meanwhile Bouchard strived to pacify Echevarria, his conciliatory letters often composed with fragments of several languages, showing lack of fluency in any but his native French. But with each communication, the chasm widened between the two men. His own economic situation deteriorated. Money from two captured ships, an estimated 95,000 pesos, was never paid to Bouchard. And a subsequent claim by Chile against the government of Peru for 109,000 pesos was never forwarded to Echevarria. Bouchard blamed Echevarria for not helping to maintain the seaworthiness *of la Argentina* and he blamed the Argentine government in general for all his hardships dating back years to his early voyage with Admiral William Brown. For his part, Echevarria felt pressure from the various creditors' claims against *la Argentina.* After Captain Miguel Burgess, an intermediary, reported that Bouchard's family was suffering hardship without Echevarria's assistance, the break became permanent. Still, Bouchard maintained a veneer of courtesy and addressed his patron as *"my very dear sir and dear compadre."* Feeling abandoned, Norberta Bouchard decried her husband's job and possible pension, lamenting she and her daughters had nothing.[8]

Shortly after putting San Martin's troops ashore at Paracas, near Pisco, Lord Cochrane initiated the blockade of Callao with the Chilean frigates *O'Higgins* and *Lautaro* and the corvette *Indepndencia.* Poor leadership and Viceroy Pezuela's defensive mindset had rendered the Spanish fleet ineffective, and Cochrane found the Spanish flagship *Esmeralda,* a pair of brigs and numerous armed gunboats and merchant ships bottled up in Callao harbor, under the protective guns of Fortress Real Felipe and two shore batteries. Anxious for action, Cochrane carefully planned a surprise night assault on the Spaniards as he had done at Valdivia. Two columns of boats silently rowed into the harbor under cover of darkness. The 240 sailors wearing identifying blue armbands rowed past the defensive floating chain at the harbor's entrance, passing two neutral ships, *USS Macedonia* and *HMS Hyperion.* The boats glided alongside *Esmeralda.* Insurgents boarded her silently and surprised the sleeping Spanish crew. A battle ensued as Spanish sailors rained musket fire on the attackers from the yard arms and rigging, but the Chilean machetes made quick and nasty work of the Spaniards on deck and the remaining sailors either surrendered or jumped into the water. The victors began looting the ship and, discovering casks of wine, began celebrating. Lord Cochrane, who received a thigh wound in the fight, ordered the sailors to press the attack to other ships but the sailors, some now drunk, refused. Instead, they sailed the *Esmeralda* out of the harbor, sustaining some damage from the shore guns. The American *Macedonia* and British *Hyperion* also put out toward sea to avoid collateral damage, lighting lamps in their rigging, as a pre-arranged sign of their neutrality. The clever, deceptive Cochrane did the same, thereby confusing the Spanish artillery, fearful of shelling neutral vessels, and the cannonade stopped. *Esmeralda* sailed free of Callao and anchored next to *O'Higgins,* along with two captured gunboats. This assault virtually neutered the Spanish naval fighting capability. The *Esmeralda* was renamed *Valdivia,* as a Chilean warship.

Thomas Cochrane always believed he should have been appointed commander-in-chief of the expedition. San Martin had offered Cochrane to become admiral of a new Peruvian navy, but Cochrane declined, staying loyal to Chile. His resentment of San Martin would soon erupt. When San Martin declined to pay expenses or prize money for the capture of the *Esmeralda,* claiming it was rather the responsibility of the Chilean government, Cochrane's fury exploded. He seized the shipment of Peruvian treasury assets that San Martin had appropriated – possibly for his own use – and distributed some of the funds to his seamen and others with claims that had not been paid. He then set out to sea on an independent mission to search and destroy any remaining Spanish ships of war. Cochrane found his prey at Guayaquil and captured a pair of frigates. In response, San Martin created an independent Peruvian navy and Hipolito Bouchard was given command of the captured 50-gun Spanish frigate *Prueba,* with the rank of graduated ship's captain. Bouchard now contemplated the possibility of confrontation with his nemesis Cochrane on the high seas. Off Callao, Cochrane cautiously approached. The two confronted each other, Bouchard even challenging the renegade admiral to a duel. Cochrane, seeing Bouchard and the Peruvians ready for action, demurred and moved away.

In his autobiography, Lord Cochrane fails to acknowledge Bouchard and downplays the incident:

> *"[We] anchored at Callao, where we found the Prueba under Peruvian colours and commanded by the senior Chilean captain, who had abandoned our squadron! To calm their fears I wrote to the Government that there was no intention of taking her, otherwise I would have done so."* [9]

Cochrane returned to Valparaiso, resigned his commission in a fit of recrimination and left the service of Chile in November 1822. In his autobiography, Lord Cochrane provided this justification for his actions:

> *"I cannot reproach myself with having done any wrong in the seizure of the money of the Protectoral Government. General San Martin and myself had been, in our respective departments, deputed to liberate Peru from Spain, and to give the Peruvians the same free institutions which Chili herself enjoyed. The first part of our object had been fully effected by the achievements and vigilance of the squadron; the second part was frustrated by General San Martin arrogating to himself despotic power, which set at naught the wishes and voice of the people...I did all in my power to warn General San Martin of the consequences of ambition so-ill-directed, but the warning was neglected, if not despised....Seeing that no intention existed on the part of the Protector's Government to do justice to the Chilian squadron, whilst every effort was made to excite discontent among the officers and men with the purpose of procuring their transfer to Peru, I seized the public money, satisfied the men, and saved the navy to the Chilian Republic, which afterwards warmly thanked me for what I had done."* [10]

About the same time, Jose de San Martin met with Simon Bolivar at Guayaquil to discuss the removal of the last bastion of royal power and the chaotic situation of trying to govern the various factions within Peru. San Martin advocated for a strong centralized government, while Bolivar was insistent on a republic. Knowing Bolivar would never assent to sharing power, the more modest San Martin resigned his position as Protector of Peru and returned to Argentina. His retirement to France followed soon after. Bolivar and his collaborator Antonio Jose de Sucre, in command of a large army, launched a final offensive in the Peruvian highlands and achieved a decisive victory over royalists in December 1824 at the Battle of Ayacucho. Among the soldiers in the battle were the *granadero* horse cavalry, Bouchard's old unit. The republican Bolivar soon assumed almost dictatorial powers in Peru.

Captain Bouchard remained in uniform for Peru, eventually being placed in command of his former ship, *Santa Rosa,* transporting troops. (Bouchard's other ship, the *Consecuecia/la Argentina* had finally been declared unfit and scrapped for firewood). On February 5, 1824, garrisoned Chilean-Argentine troops staged an uprising and handed the fortress at Callao back over to royalists. Bouchard was called to blockade the harbor and cannonade the uprising on shore. During the action, the *Santa Rosa* was retaken by royalists, and, in a subsequent effort to rescue her, she was burned rather than given over to the enemy. In a report to Bolivar, Antonio Gutierrez de la Fuente, later briefly supreme head of Peru, singled out Bouchard for bravery.

In 1828, border issues, the collapse of the proposed federation of Bolivia, Peru and Colombia, and general controversy over the administration of Bolivar erupted into an internecine war between Peru and Gran-Colombia (modern Colombia, Venezuela, Ecuador and Panama). The Peruvian corvette *Libertad* was attacked by a pair of Gran-Colombian warships off Punta Malpelo and Peruvian admiral Martin Guisse was killed in the fierce battle. Sixteen Peruvian warships and transports, including the frigate *Presidente,* began a blockade of the entire Gran-Colombian Pacific Coast. Bouchard would write to his younger brother Hippolyte in France:

> *"After a long battle at the fort of Guayaquil, unfortunately the frigate Presidente that I was sailing took fire and seeing that there were no means to save it as a result of another explosion, I transferred over to Libertad where I am commander of the squadron."* [11]

Following the death of Admiral Guisse, Bouchard was elevated to Admiral in charge of the Peruvian navy, the apex of his career. A year later, carless crew were responsible for a fire aboard *Libertad.* Bouchard was scapegoated for the loss of the ship, reduced in rank back down to captain and retired.

At this later stage of his life, Bouchard maintained correspondence with his siblings in Europe. Before his appointment as admiral, he had contemplated returning to France – perhaps even joining San Martin in retirement there. He anticipated that after peace was declared, Lima would award him all the money he was owed, an estimated 300,000 piastres – and that would be sufficient for him to return to France and support his brothers there. His siblings were both military veterans, one in the Grand Armee and the other had followed Andre-Paul into the French navy. Clearly, he no longer harbored any thoughts of returning to Argentina. His marriage was bankrupt, though he corresponded sporadically with his daughters, and named his last ship *Joven Fermina* (Young Fermina) after the daughter he never knew.[12]

Bouchard worried about selling all assets, including his ship *Joven Fermina,* to finance his retirement. Instead, the Peruvian government offered him two *haciendas in* the Nazca hinterlands south of Lima. Despite counterclaims against Bouchard, including by Vicente Echevarria over rights to *la Argentina* and *Santa Rosa,* the Peruvian congress approved the land grant. [13]

Still dressed in his naval uniform and carrying his saber, the overland trek from the port at Pisco, across barren desert must have seemed foreign to someone who had spent his life at sea. The old Inca Way passed through the mountains before opening to a green oasis along the banks of the Rio Grande River. Adjacent to a small adobe village stood the massive façade of the Church of San Javier and the hacienda Bouchard would call home.

The *ranchos* at San Javier and San Jose de la Nazca had been established by 17th century Jesuits on their mission to Christianize the indigenous people of the Rio Grande de Nazca River basin. Adjacent to the r*anchos* the pre-Inca Nazca natives had carved giant geoglyphs into the stony desert surface more than a thousand years earlier. These giant images of plants and animals, some more than thirty miles in length, incorporating straight lines, geometrical patterns, spirals, waves and zigzags, may have had astronomical or calendar functions, or been directional markers or religious symbols. Still today, these remarkable shapes, plainly visible from the air, remain a mystery – and allow some to theorize about their association with ancient alien astronauts. As a lifelong sailor, not a farmer, Bouchard now faced the challenge of making his existence at one of the driest areas on earth.

With his typical determination, Bouchard endeavored to make a success of his estates, growing cotton, sugarcane and muscat grapes from which he distilled *pisco* (brandy). The hard agricultural work and harvesting cycles gave some predictability to Bouchard's life. However, the arid conditions and great distance from the nearest port at Pisco worked against him. Along with the *haciendas*, he had inherited several hundred slaves who were essential to the working of the plantation. One of the great ironies of Bouchard's life is that the egalitarian who was repulsed by what he saw in Saint Domingue and who brought cannons to bear on the slave ships at Tamatave, now was slave master. With the same firmness he displayed with his crews on board ship, Bouchard now tasked his slaves with hard labor and meted out harsh punishment for those who lagged.

Revolutionary leaders called for the abolition of slavery to be gradual, without much impact on current slave owners. With the slave trade banned in 1812, it was thought slavery would die a natural death with time. But enslaved peoples clamored for immediate freedom. Many achieved emancipation by enlisting in the revolutionary army. Although the revolution weakened slavery in South America, it would continue in practice for several decades.

In the volatile politics of the new nation, a *coup d'etat* against the Provisional President of the Peruvian Republic, Luis Jose de Orbegoso by Felipe Salaverry resulted in the call for hundreds of slaves to be conscripted into the rebel army. In a move to protect his workers and deny the rebels the fighters, Bouchard dispersed his slaves into the surrounding mountains. Upon their return, many of the slaves, having tasted a degree of freedom, were no longer willing to work as before. They complained about working conditions and petitioned a local judge at Ica to improve their benefits. Additionally, they lobbied the serious issue of supposedly being denied access to a chaplain and the holy sacraments at the Bouchard *ranchos*. Bouchard reacted to the insubordination as he had to mutiny on his ships and offered no quarter. An indentured Afro-Nazi (mixed indigenous Nazca) manager named Adelfo Bernales saw an opportunity to be rid of the overbearing Frenchman for good and plotted with others. On January 4, 1837, five slaves waited in hiding before attacking the master and brutally killing him. A rumor – never confirmed – claimed he died cradled in the arms of his slave mistress while his assailants danced around his bloody corpse. Nor did a rumored son ever come forward. For many years the local people of Nazca would repeat the chant, "We killed Bucha." According to a death certificate registered by Fr. Isidro Caceres, he was hastily buried in the crypt of San Francisco Javier on his own property. He never received the last rights of his church.

At age 57, Hipolito Bouchard may have anticipated nearing the end. He had ceased trying to repay his debts years before. The government had been trying to repossess his *ranchos.* He had indicated all his possessions should go to his daughters, though he had not executed a will. But all that remained were two trunks of military uniforms and civilian clothes, dictionaries of naval terminology and of Spanish, a book of Christian meditations and one on natural history, and the *Ordinances of the Royal Spanish Navy governing all of Spanish America.* His sword was not in the inventory of his possessions that would later be returned to his family. It would remain for posterity to remember and reconcile the legacy of this French revolutionary, adopted patriot of three nations and one of the last great privateers of the age of sail.

Notes:

1. Peter Corney, Voyages in the Northern Pacific, Honolulu, HI: Thos. Thrum, Publisher, 1896, pp. 126-127.
2. Thomas Cochrane, correspondence to Chilean Minister of the Navy, July 11, 1819.
3. Hipolito Bouchard in Miguel Angel DeMarco, "Recien hace unos anos, un juez de EEUU absolvo a Bouchard de pirateria," interview with Claudia Peiro, *infobae,* October 27, 2018, http//www.infobae.com>2018/10/27, retrieved September 14, 2022.
4. Thomas Cochrane, Narrative of the Services in the Liberation of Chili, Peru and Brazil from Spanish and Portuguese Domination, vol. 1 (1858), A Public Domain Book, 2012, electronic version, not paginated.
5. Court decision, *Copy of the Process of Captain Hipolito Bouchard,* Department of Naval Historical Studies, vol. V, Buenos Aires, 1987.
6. Peter Corney, op. cit., p. 127.
7. Ibid.
8. Miguel Angel DeMarco, Halcon de los Mares. Corsario de la Libertad, Buenos Aires,: Emece, 2018, pp.216-224.
9. Thomas Cochrane, op. cit.
10. Thomas Cochrane, op. cit.
11. Miguel Angel DeMarco, op cit., p. 223-224.
12. Ibid. pp. 224-225.
13. Ibid.

Epilogue

"He who serves a revolution ploughs a sea."

–Simon Bolivar

"Don't Cry for Me, Argentina"

–Tim Rice and Andrew Lloyd Webber, *Evita* (1976)

The ideas of the Enlightenment which had inflamed the North American patriots to break with England and which fueled revolution in France and underpinned the successful revolt of enslaved thousands in Saint Domingue, also found fertile ground among the *criollos* of Spanish America as they questioned their allegiance to Spain. After three decades of war, as much among themselves as against a common Spanish foe, the Latin-*Americanos* prevailed. By 1833, the Spanish-American wars of independence were over. The once mighty Spanish Empire, which had conquered and exploited its American colonies for 300 years, had been stripped of its holdings from Cape Mendocino to Cape Horn. In the western hemisphere only Cuba and Puerto Rico remained part of Spain.

In the aftermath of war, the former South American colonies were left to self-government, devolving into an almost permanent pattern of authoritarian rule, military dictatorships, and a stratified political and economic system where power remained in the hands of the elite, and which, to an extent, perpetuates today. And while Spain was expelled, its influence and language remained, along with the spiritual and social domination of the Roman Catholic Church. While no longer enslaved and forced to exploit the resources of the New World, indigenous people, nevertheless remained marginalized and mixed-race *mestizos* often suffered harsh discrimination.

Charles C. Griffin summarized his hypothesis on the effects of independence thus:

> *"The revolutionary wars which led to independence were a profound shock to the society and to the economic life of the Spanish colonies. Wartime destruction left many countries less able to maintain traditional ways and opened the way for new developments. Ensuing changes were brought about, first of all, by the expansion of foreign trade, which, in turn, had repercussions on the whole economic and social structure. Nevertheless, only the beginnings of a basic transformation took place and there were many ways in which colonial attitudes and institutions carried over into the life of Republican Spanish America. Liberal ideas, however, used at first to buttress the rising power of landowners and businessmen, weakened paternalistic aspects of colonialism."* [1]

Meanwhile, in 1823, the United States issued the Monroe Doctrine precluding European intervention in American affairs in either continent of the western hemisphere, along with a corresponding promise not to meddle in European affairs. It remains a cornerstone of U.S. foreign policy.

Driven south by the reduced otter population, the Russian fur trappers increasingly interacted with Mexican or American interests along the California coast. However, by 1839, increased competition from foreign trade and the inability of the farming efforts in northern California to meet the food production needs of trappers in Alaska, forced the decision to abandon Fort Ross. Mexico had refused to recognize Russian sovereignty in the region and the Russians sold the assets of the Russian American Company to rancher and entrepreneur John Sutter in 1841.

The operation fell into disuse and neglect. Following several restoration attempts, Fort Ross became a Historic Monument and part of the California State Park System in the early 20th century, comprising restored Russian structures, exhibits of Russian and Kashaya Indian life and recreation facilities, set in the redwood forest and rugged ocean coves where California's only pirates once came ashore.

Monterey continued to be the capital of California during the Mexican era. Increased American whaling interests kept California ports active. The U.S.-Mexican War, sparked by a border conflict in Texas, and used as a pretext by American Manifest Destiny expansionists for war, resulted in the Treaty of Guadalupe Hidalgo, which ceded half of Mexico, including California, to the United States in 1848. That same year, discovery of gold in California opened a torrent of Anglo immigration. The territory was quickly annexed and rushed into statehood by 1850. Monterey hosted California's first constitutional convention. Near the site of the former *presidio,* the original cathedral, spared by Bouchard, remains in contemporary use. It is the oldest stone building west of the Mississippi River. Long a center of commercial fishing until the sardine stocks were depleted by the 1950s, Monterey became a magnet for artists, poets and writers such as Robert Louis Stevenson (1879) and Nobel Laureate John Steinbeck in the 20th century, whose books *Cannery Row, Tortilla Flat* and *East of Eden,* created indelible images of the region. Today, the U.S. Defense Language Institute occupies the heights where cannons once exchanged fire with *Santa Rosa de Chacabuco,* and a monument now flies the flag of Argentina, commemorating that week in 1818. Not all citizens of Monterey are amused.

Following the Mexican era, Santa Barbara's prosperous community surrounding the original Spanish *presidio* and whaling wharves evolved into a boisterous gold rush era town; later a Victorian era health resort community, followed by an oil boom until the drilling rigs were moved offshore where they still controversially spoil the seascape and threaten the environment. Local building codes and emphasis on Spanish colonial architecture have enabled Santa Barbara to avoid the urban sprawl of southern California to become one of the most desirable – and expensive – housing markets in the state. A couple miles northwest of the old *presidio,* Mission Santa Barbara sits serene and handsomely restored, surveying the city and sea as Queen of the Missions. Refugio Beach offers recreation and a campground named for Hipolito Bouchard. After

200 years, up the narrow road into Refugio Canyon, there is no trace of the Ortega hacienda, burned during California's only pirate raids.

Nestled in the fold between the heavy development of today's Orange County and the coastal approach to the greater San Diego metropolitan area, the town of San Juan Capistrano promotes its colorful history and mission heritage, while trying to withstand the pressures of tourism. Dozens of restored 19th century buildings surround the original mission complex, now fully restored. Mission San Juan Capistrano has served continuously as an operating church since its founding in 1786, tenth in the chain of California missions.

In 1826, the first native Mexican, elected governor of Alta California issued a *Proclamacion de Emancipacion,* freeing all Indians from the military districts of Monterey, Santa Barbara and San Diego from missions' rule. The following year, the Mexican government deported from Alta California all residents of Spanish birth younger than 60 years of age. After secularization of the mission system in 1834, Mexican authority was further decentralized, as the former mission lands fell to private ownership of a few wealthy *Californios.* The indigenous Indian population was no longer served by the mission or rancho economies.

At San Juan Capistrano, cycles of flood, drought, cattle disease and weed infestation reduced the mission and grounds to a state of decay and rendered the mission barely functional as a parish church. In 1845, Governor Pio Pico sold the mission complex at public auction to his brother-in-law Don Juan (John) Forster for $710 (about $16,000 in today's money – a steal!) In 1865, President Abraham Lincoln, in one of his last acts before being assassinated, deeded the mission back to the Church. Serious restoration did not take place until the 20th century. After years of failed efforts due to lack of masonry construction expertise, restoration on the Great Stone Church, minus the original Greco Roman dome, which collapsed in the earthquake of 1812, was completed only in 2004.

Today the adjacent Serra Chapel, looted by the insurgents, claims to be the oldest standing building in California. The restored buildings and gardens, including California's first winery, and a museum showcasing paintings and artifacts hidden from the pirates, tell the mission's story. Beautifully restored, San Juan Capistrano brands itself as *Jewel of the California Missions.* It took Hipolito Bouchard a voyage of almost two years to arrive at San Juan Capistrano. Today, migrating swallows make the long flight from Argentina to the mission each spring in three weeks. As at many of the missions, the cemetery claims the remains of some 4,000 Native Americans – likely a very conservative estimate. Though no evidence of treasure buried during the pirate raid has ever surfaced, legends continue to motivate treasure hunters.

Dana Point, at the tip of Capistrano Bay, has become a popular surfing location and a monument marks the landing of Bouchard. In the 1950's, a heavily deteriorated cannon of late 18th century design was discovered in the sand of Dana Point's Doheny Cove. The small-bore weapon appears to be a portable swivel gun used for firing grapeshot. Archeological evidence and the historical record all point toward this artifact likely being left behind as Bouchard's drunken sailors returned to their ships after rampaging at San Juan Capistrano. The cannon is currently on display at the Bowers Museum in Santa Ana, California.

And what of the actors in our drama? None created a larger impact and left a greater legacy than **Simon Bolivar,** *el Libetador.* Often referred to as "the George Washington of South America," Latin Americans are quick to point out that while Washington liberated one colonial nation from tyranny, Bolivar liberated six. By any measure, he is South America's greatest hero and patriot. He succeeded in uniting much of a continent but the governments he established were fragile. He believed only authoritarian governments could be strong enough to administer such large, diverse countries. He said, *"A single government may use its great resources [to] lift us to the summit of power and prosperity."* As Dictator of Peru, he oversaw the creation of Bolivia and hoped Peru, Columbia and Bolivia would unite. But internal forces pressed for separate nations and the dream of unity dissolved into civil war by 1826. His creation of Gran Colombia splintered when his native Venezuela left the union, followed by Ecuador. Years later Panama would also divorce from Colombia. Frustrated, angry and dejected, Bolivar resigned his positions in 1830 with plans to retire in Europe, but lingering illness, probably tuberculosis, claimed the life of the Liberator in December of that year in Santa Marta, Gran Colombia. His remains were first reinterred with his parents and wife in Venezuela, before finally put to rest in the Venezuelan National Pantheon in Caracas.

Revered and even offered kingship, Bolivar was also despised as a tyrant and criticized as a bourgeois revolutionary and half-hearted reformer. Yet his enduring life of adventure, tragedy and glory are remembered with his namesake nation of Bolivia and numerous cities, towns, statues, paintings, histories, dramas and much more, in ways most heroes in history have never been.

Marie Arana concludes her great biography of Bolivar by writing,

> *"Here is an all too imperfect man...Here is a leader whom fate presented with one opportunity and a glut of insuperable hurdles...With a stamina that is arguably unmatched in history, he prosecuted a seemingly unwinnable war over the harshest of terrains to shuck the formidable banner of [conquistador] Pizarro. From Haiti to Potosi, there was little that stopped him. On he rode, into the void, fighting against unimaginable odds. Until he remade a world."* [2]

Only slightly obscured by the brilliance reflecting from Bolivar is the other great liberating hero of South American independence, **Jose de San Martin.** Historians still wonder what transpired between San Martin and Simon Bolivar at their meeting in Guayaquil. But by 1824, San Martin had unexpectedly resigned his command of the army, returned briefly to Argentina and sailed off to France in early retirement, leaving Bolivar to complete the liberation of Peru San Martin had started. Recently widowed following the death of his wife, Remedios de Escalada, San Martin and his daughter, Mercedes Tomasa, moved to France, then Britain, next Belgium, always planning to return to Argentina. From across the Atlantic he feuded with the unitarians and took the part of the federalists in the politics of de la Plata. A return to South America was aborted when San Martin found the unitarians firmly in charge upon his arrival at Buenos Aires and he never disembarked. He received no response to his offer of services to Brazil and the Argentine federalist dictator Juan Manuel de Rosas also declined San Martin's offer due to his age. During the 1848 uprising in France,

San Martin relocated from Paris to the northern city of Boulogne-sur-mer, where he maintained a steady correspondence with friends in South America until his eyes failed. This other great Father of South American independence died in 1850. San Martin's remains were repatriated to Argentina 30 years later. The seven remaining living veterans of *his Granaderos de Caballo* met the ship at the dock upon arrival and accompanied the transfer of their leader's remains to the Cathedral in Buenos Aires. Years later his old regiment was reactivated and now each day a symbolic seven soldiers march from the Casa Rosada presidential palace to the Cathedral, where a pair of *granaderos st*and guard at San Martin's tomb.

San Martin is venerated as a national hero in Argentina, Chile and Peru. His achievement in taking his army across the Andes remains unmatched in modern military history.

John Lynch, the emeritus professor of Latin American History at University of London and San Martin biographer, describes San Martin as a migrant who returned home to find the doors closed. He writes,

> *"In the South American revolution San Martin led with his ideas and his actions, taking the revolution outside national frontiers and beyond national interests and giving it an American identity,"* Lynch goes on to echo Argentine historian Bartolome Mitre who called San Martin *"the American man, the necessary man."* [3]

The great men (and women) of history seldom come in pairs. Perhaps Lincoln and Grant or Roosevelt and Churchill. Despite their differences, history shows that Bolivar and San Martin were ultimately complimentary. Neither could have effected the liberation of the South American continent by themselves. Hipolito Bouchard was never a deep intellectual political theorist, nor great military strategist, but he held the values of the revolution deep to his core. He instinctively recognized the inherent greatness of these two leaders and without hesitation rallied to their flag and their cause.

Among the major figures of the Spanish-American wars of independence not receiving Bouchard's admiration was his nemesis,

Admiral **Thomas Cochrane.** After resigning his Chilean commission, bitter over perceived slights and the failure of both Chile and Peru to reward him properly, Cochrane planned to return to England. However, still barred from his former political and naval career in Britain, Cochrane instead accepted the offer from Brazil to assume command of their navy in their own war of independence from Portugal in 1823. After Napoleon had invaded Portugal, the Portuguese royal family had fled to Brazil, establishing the Brazilian Empire under Emperor Pedro I. With customary skill and daring, Cochrane, as First Admiral of the National and Imperial Navy, succeeded in destroying the Portuguese fleet, making Brazil free of foreign troops and largely independent. He was rewarded with the title of marquess. However, once again Cochrane quarreled with the government over pay and prize money as well as perceived plots against him. In 1824, while sailing to quell a republican revolt in the northern provinces of Brazil, he absconded with money from the treasury just as he had done in Peru and transferred to a frigate bound for Britain. He next found employment aiding Greece in its attempts at liberation from the Ottoman Empire, with limited results.

Cochrane inherited his title as 10th Earl of Dundonald and received a royal pardon in 1832. He eventually had his knighthood in the Order of the Bath restored by Queen Victoria in 1847. He was restored to service in the Royal Navy, received a series of rapid promotions to Admiral rank and became Honorary Rear Admiral of the United Kingdom, though considered too old and unpredictable for a command in the Baltic during the Crimean War. Together with writer G.B. Earp, he penned a pair of self-serving autobiographies about his career before dying during kidney stone surgery in 1860. He is buried in a prominent location in Westminster Abbey, London.

In 1857, the Chilean government offered a settlement of full pay at his rank for life in gratitude for

> *"the taking of Valdivia, the feats at Callao, the bloody and splendid triumph of the Esmeralda, the taking of the Spanish frigates Prueba and Venganza on the coast of Ecuador and the complete annihilation of the power of Spain in these seas executed by our squadron under the command of Lord Cochrane."* [4]

Ever the negotiator and best self-advocate, Lord Dundonald replied:

> *"I must be permitted to observe that the grant of full pay, on prospectively, to one who is upwards of eighty years of age, is little more than nominal, as my life, in all human probability, is approaching its close...I therefore beg most respectfully to suggest to the consideration of your Excellency, to that of the Council and National Congress [of Chile], as well as to the just feeling of the honorable people of Chili, that one half of the pay which I received in actual service, be accorded to me retrospectively [retroactively] in the same manner that a similar boon was granted by the Brazilian nation."* [5]

Though his claims against the South American nations he helped liberate were never satisfactorily resolved, he is nevertheless remembered each May with a wreath on his tomb laid by the Chilean Navy. In addition to his supreme naval skills, Cochrane was an accomplished engineer with several patents. He designed a tunnel shield for the pedestrian walkway under the Thames River and was an early proponent of steam powered warships. Only time and cost overruns prevented ships of his design from joining his fleets. He is obviously the inspiration and model for the *Horatio Hornblower* books by E.S. Forester and the *Aubrey-Maturin* series by Patrick O'Brian, which led to the film *Master and Commander,* though, in truth, art's attempts to imitate life fall short of the brilliant real-life exploits and adventures of one of Britain's and America's greatest naval heroes.

Another admiral of note with whom Bouchard had a disagreeable relationship was **William Brown**. After their unfriendly separation in the Galapagos Islands, Brown continued to harass Spanish shipping along the Pacific coast before returning to Argentina. However, off Montevideo, Uruguay, he feared Spanish and Portuguese interception and sailed on to the West Indies. The British Navy suspected Brown of privateering and ordered him to Barbados, where he was stripped of his ship and valuable plunder. He sailed on to London and after a lengthy appeals process was exonerated, only to face another trial in Buenos Aires over his decision to sail to the Pacific contrary to the orders of the government. After a forced retirement he was called back into service during a three-year war with Brazil over Uruguay. Brown's successful campaigns against the Brazilians led toward the eventual peace and recognition of an independent Uruguay in 1828. Grateful Argentines chose Brown to be governor of Buenos Aires, but his democratic initiatives were blunted, and General Juan Manuel de Rosas became dictator. Brown was called from retirement for a third time when combined British, French and United States forces blockaded Argentina. During the conflict, Brown destroyed a squadron under the Italian Giuseppe Garibaldi (later to become the Father of Italian Unification). Foes in battle, the two became close friends. Garibaldi considered Brown the greatest naval officer of his era. Brown lived quietly in Buenos Aires and spent some time in his native Ireland before dying in 1857. At his funeral, Brown was described as worth more as one man than an entire fleet of ships. The Father of the Argentine Navy is buried in Recoleta Cemetery in Buenos Aires. Memorials abound throughout Argentina, as well as Ireland. Argentine admirals wear a replica of *Almirante* Guillermo Brown's sword.

As for the crew who sailed with Bouchard, less is known. **Ramon Freire Serrano (1787-1851)**, who was a deck officer on Bouchard's earlier voyage with William Brown, traded the deck of a ship for an army commission, accompanying San Martin over the Andes. Freire went on to become president of Chile on four separate occasions, but never managed to consolidate his power. Political infighting drove him into exile in Tahiti and Australia, before returning to Chile where he died in 1851. The liberal Chilean Constitution of 1828 satisfied nobody and despite swings of the political pendulum, the government stayed in the hands of the elite throughout the 19th century.

Tomas Espora, who survived the long Pacific voyage with Bouchard and loyally testified on his behalf at his piracy trial, advanced his career in the Chilean navy, becoming *comandante general de marina* in 1833 and *comandante en jefe de la escuadrilla* (commander in chief of the fleet) in 1834, before dying young in 1835.

One American crewman from Bouchard's fleet became one of the first American-born permanent residents of Alta California. A New Englander called **Joseph John Chapman** may have been one of the mutineers that tried to sell *Santa Rosa* to King Kamehameha when Bouchard arrived in Hawai'i. He either agreed or was impressed to serve on Bouchard's crew. Chapman was one of three sailors captured on the beach at Monterey Bay and later released. He was captured again on the raid of the Ortega hacienda at Refugio. Alternately, he may have deserted Bouchard and asked for asylum from the Spaniards at Santa Barbara. Held under arrest until Mexican independence in 1821, Chapman converted to Catholicism, married Maria Guadalupe, daughter of Don Jose Ortega, and became a Mexican citizen known as Jose Juan Chapman y Cananta. A skilled blacksmith, carpenter and medical practitioner, Chapman was well-known throughout southern California. Eventually he and his family moved to Santa Barbara, where he died in 1849 and was buried in the mission cemetery.

Much of what we know of Bouchard's voyage along the coast of North America comes from the publication of **Peter Corney's** serialized memoir, *Voyages in the Northern Pacific; Narrative of Several Trading Voyages from 1813 to 1818.* Based on his familiarity with the Russian fur trade and the Spanish *presidios* in Alta California, it was Corney who convinced Bouchard to sail from Hawai'i to America in search of Spanish plunder. After Corney quit as captain of *Santa Rosa de Chacabuco* in Valparaiso in 1819, he left empty handed and returned to England., where he married Frances Loder in Cork, Ireland the following year. Corney reestablished his connections in the Pacific northwest, sailing out as chief mate on another ship named *Columbia (*there were at least four vessels so named), making the run between the Oregon Territory and Canton, via Hawai'i. Corney correctly warned that Britain must not be complacent about dominance in the northwest Pacific, given the rising power of the United States. In 1835, accompanied by his wife and four children aboard a ship out from Gravesend, England, Corney died while still in the English Channel. The ship was bound for Hawai'i.

In Buenos Aires, entrepreneur investor **Vicente Anastasio Echevarria,** who had been integral to the First Triumvirate of the independence movement before turning to commercial interests, never relented in seeking compensation from Hipolito Bouchard for *la Argentina.* He died in 1857 and is buried in la Recoleta. Despite differences between their husbands, Echevarria's wife, **Maria Antonia,** remained friends with **Norberta Merlo de Bouchard.**

In Alta California, **Governor Pablo Vicente de Sola** weathered the criticism about his strategic retreat in the face of Bouchard's raiders. In time, he became congratulated for a strategy of saving lives and items of value. A Spanish-born monarchist who violently opposed the nascent independence movement, Sola nevertheless acquiesced to the fact of Mexican independence and remained governor during the initial transition to Mexican rule until 1822. He was the last Spanish born and last Spanish appointed governor of Alta California, and first under the Mexican flag. A strong advocate of education, he established schools at the *presidios* and personally financed the education of young *Californios.* He died In Mexico City in 1826.

Most of what we know about **Hipolito Bouchard,** himself, we must infer from the works of others and from his own actions. A native-born Frenchman with only basic schooling and a provincial accent, Bouchard was a man of deeds rather than words. The few surviving letters and reports that he wrote are tersely composed and written in a kind of pidgin Spanish, incorporating words or phrases from a variety of languages – not surprising given the polyglot makeup of his crews. The references found in the writing of others tend to reflect that writer's point of view – Sola, for example, or Cochrane – and must be evaluated as much for spin as for history. Perhaps Peter Corney's reflections best capture Bouchard's adventures, but only from the point of view of someone who sailed under him, and they only address the period from Hawai'i to arrival at Valparaiso. And Corney's narrative skips over large chunks of time and detail.

Much of the detail of Bouchard's life remains unknown. For all its adventure and drama, the arc of his life was very linear. From youth, he was drawn to the sea. He enlisted in the French Navy and spent the rest of his life on the water, except for a brief period as a land-based soldier in Argentina and his final years as a farmer in

Peru. Sailing was the life he knew, performed best, and, we assume, enjoyed most. For Bouchard, being a mariner satisfied three objectives: it provided him with a marketable occupation from which to make his living; it provided the outlet for him to express his revolutionary impulses in wars of independence; and thirdly, it offered upward mobility and accumulation of wealth in a very stratified society.

From his earliest days as a gunnery seaman on French warships, Bouchard took to life onboard a vessel. When command was thrust upon him in Argentina, he rebounded from disaster and gained the self-confidence and skill to captain a ship. His initial Pacific expedition with Admiral William Brown was an overall success. His subsequent round-the-world voyage on *la Argentina* was epic. His was not a voyage of discovery, cultural awakening nor scientific breakthrough. Nor was he the first navigator to sail those waters and visit those lands. But his accomplishments of seamanship, survival and determination place him in the conversation with Magellan, Drake, Cook and only a few others. His prowess as a ship's captain cannot be measured in number of ships taken or sunk, though he did that. Not quantified in harbors blockaded or enemy ports raided, and he did that as well. Rather it is a story of raw grit in the face of nature's fury and a powerful enemy that would have capsized a weaker sailor and scuttled his ship.

As a revolutionary, Bouchard was largely one dimensional. Imbued with revolutionary zeal from childhood, he walked the walk of *liberte, egalite, fraternite.* Leave it for others such as Voltaire or Rousseau to talk the talk; Bouchard was all about putting thoughts into action. He was no propagandist, interested in turning mass public opinion toward independence. Nor would he be found in a tavern or *pulperia* arguing about the subtilties of revolution. He spoke freedom from the muzzle of a 12 pounder and vowed death to those who disagreed. He was anti-monarchist and saw the reactionary forces in Europe as counterrevolutionary. He championed Napoleon until the French Republic morphed into the Empire of Bonaparte, belying the values of the Revolution. He seemed surprised that the populace of Alta California did not rise in rebellion on his arrival. Perhaps that was naïve. The largely uneducated people in the mission and *presidio* environment had never been introduced to ideas of freedom, and besides they had not stayed around to have that conversation with the aggressive pirates on a seek-and-destroy mission. Nor did Bouchard possess the charisma of a revolutionary leader who could inspire dangerous insurrection. Rather, he identified with those leaders who could articulate those revolutionary ideas and lead men into battle for the cause. Instead, Bouchard represented the most loyal of followers, the most passionate and able of the foot soldiers of the revolution.

Where Bouchard eventually diverges from his revolutionary values is, of course, on the issue of race. The European attitudes of racial superiority had been transplanted to the Americas. The noble ideals of the Enlightenment did not transcend the inherent racism in society. Slavery remained a fabric of society in one form or another until long after the colonies of both North and South America achieved independence from their mother countries. Only the most ardent abolitionists ever called for immediate emancipation. And in the elaborate *casta* system, one's place in society was predetermined by the shade of skin coloration or drops of racial blood. From the onset, Bouchard abhorred the notion of slavery. He was scarred by what he witnessed on Saint Domingue. He physically freed slaves on Madagascar and enlisted former slaves, along with sailors of all nationalities, to crew his ships. While he may have privately held racially prejudiced thoughts, there's no indication that he practiced any discrimination toward his crew. Yet in the end, it was slavery that proved his undoing. Most likely that was due to economic rather than racial factors. In lieu of money, Peru had rewarded Bouchard with property, including slaves to work the *rancho*. Without slaves there would be no income. Bouchard was caught in a bind. In the end, Bouchard fell victim to the system he hated.

Bouchard's third objective was material wealth. From his arrival in Buenos Aires to his last days at Nazca, he was obsessed with obtaining wealth and the status it conveyed. For a sailor, the options were limited. Only ships' officers and owners received more than a subsistence wage. Bouchard, as captain, stood to make a significant sum. It was common practice among navies of the world to capture and sell enemy ships, along with any cargoes. Senior officers and national treasuries could benefit nicely from successful naval campaigns. Smaller shares were distributed to the crews as a form of motivation; however, these sums were often quickly dissipated in the harbor taverns and brothels or gambled away. As privateers augmented national navies, entrepreneurs also saw income opportunities. Despite the risks, income potential was huge as was the return on investment for the patrons who bought and outfitted the ships. Bouchard saw privateering for the revolution as a lucrative way to fight the good fight and advance in society. In the end, it didn't pay out so well. After two years of voyage, Bouchard had very little to show for his efforts. They had lost more ships than they had gained; the targets of their raids had removed anything of value before their arrival; and after his incarceration in Chile, Bouchard was left with only empty ships. Even his ships represented a loss as the *Santa Rosa* burned and *la Argentina* rotted and was scrapped. With no money, Bouchard was unable to repay his debts, or return to Argentina and he ultimately died land-poor.

Privateering realized its last surge during the American wars of independence. Increasingly the distinction between privateering and piracy blurred. Whether a ship was authorized to plunder seemed to make little difference. Neutral shipping was at risk as well as vessels from hostile nations. With no agreed-upon international standards, privateering had become a sea-born plague. Because it had become nearly impossible to distinguish between legal and unlawful search and seizure on the high seas, the practice of private confiscation of ships and booty was condemned and abolished by the 1856 Declaration of Paris. Though the practice continued in defiance of international law, privateering, now equated with piracy, ebbed away.[6]

The discussion about whether Hipolito Bouchard was a pirate or a privateer borders on the semantic and should probably be put to rest. The distinction between the two terms has become so blurred as to be almost meaningless. Judging history in its own time and space leads us to conclude that Bouchard thought he was a privateer. The United Provinces government issued a letter of marque (several) which they believed to be valid and accepted by other nations. The fact that United Provinces had not been recognized diplomatically by other nations complicates the issue. But most other nations at the time understood that there was legitimate sanctioned privateering as opposed to unauthorized piracy and accepted the fact. That Bouchard ran out the clock on his letter of marque before the California raids is a technicality that changes none of the facts as they happened. If that switched gears from privateering to piracy, then so be it. Bouchard was absolved of piracy by the Chilean court. As late as 1988 an American judge in a mock trial declared that Bouchard's actions had not been those of a pirate; that he acted in the interests of a free country at war with another. But pirates make for a better story.

The marriage of Hipolito Bouchard is a troubling story, though perhaps not unusual with men who go down to the sea. He married the young Norberta de Merlo as a means to integrate into the strict society of Buenos Aires. Perhaps they were in love. He fathered two daughters then embarked on a voyage, never to return. The presence of his wife's two brothers on board his ship would have been a daily reminder of her. For two years she had no communication of her husband's location or fate. When he arrived back in South American waters he intended to return to Buenos Aires; perhaps the family would have reunited. However, his dire financial situation and vulnerability to creditors back in Buenos Aires led him to choose otherwise. The pull of a salary and to continue the fight for independence in Peru proved too strong. Norberta despaired the lack of support for her family. In 1819, Bouchard sat for a portrait by the Peruvian artist Jose Gil de Castro. He was painted wearing a plain blue naval uniform. On his little finger he is shown wearing a small ring inscribed with his wife's initials. Many years later, in 1835, Bouchard again sat for de Castro for another portrait, this time wearing the full-dress uniform of a Peruvian captain. He wears the Chilean Legion of Merit and the Army and Squadron Liberators of Peru medals. Around his neck he is shown wearing the Order of the Sun decoration, Peru's highest honor (Created by San Martin to invoke the great Inca Empire, the medallion was also awarded to Chilean hero Bernardo O'Higgins and San Martin, himself. Lord Cochrane, no stranger to honors, refused it, chiding San Martin for arrogance and pomp). In the second portrait, the matured Bouchard no longer wears the ring. The marriage is long broken, but, of course, as good Catholics, there is no divorce.

In 1822, political turmoil caused many families to leave Buenos Aires. With the help of Vicente Echevarria, Bouchard's wife and daughters relocated to Montevideo. Sometime after Bouchard's death, Norberta possibly shed her black widow's weeds and may have remarried. She continually pressed for some sort of government assistance. In 1864, Argentine President and historian Bartolome Mitre wrote an article about Hipolito Bouchard for the *Revista (Magazine) de Buenos Aires.*

Encouraged by the article and citing her "sad circumstances," Norberta wrote to the president:

> *"The services of my late husband rendered to the cause of America are of notoriety and no one better than your excellency recognizes them by making them public through the work that his skillful pen has written with such industriousness."*

But demands on the national treasury precluded any help.

Senora de Bouchard suffered from chronic nosebleeds for the rest of her life. She died in 1869, perhaps having seen the 1819 portrait of her husband as she remembered him. Efforts to have their father recognized and to receive some survivor's benefit continued by both daughters. In 1872, Carmen, who had never married, received a small stipend. An inheritance trial later bogged down into a debate about whether Bouchard had been a regular commissioned soldier or simply a privateer. Old resentments about his failing to return to Argentina resurfaced and the efforts for compensation stalled. Daughter Fermina had married Lucas Fernandez des Ramos, of a prominent Uruguayan family, and raised nine children. She died in 1886.[7]

His family relations aside, Hipolito Bouchard would have been a difficult man to know. He seems to have cultivated few friends. Among his crews, some admired or respected his leadership, but many hated him. Some refused to sail with him. A couple tried to kill him. He was a stern, even mean disciplinarian, who coolly meted out punishment and met disrespect and hostility with a pistol or whip. He was calloused about death of his crew members and certainly didn't think twice about the enemy. He likely had no real fear of his own death, at sea or in battle. He was uncommonly brave, even to the point of recklessness, virtues some may have admired but many did not. He curried the favor of those in power and basked in the reflected glory of others. But many soon tired of his arrogance and erratic behavior, and financial or political support melted away. In an environment that rewarded culture, he was found lacking. His manners, like his large frame, seemed awkward and course. He was not above lying, forging documents or otherwise deceiving to accomplish his ends. Yet he did hold fast to the principles he believed in, and he adhered to accepted rules of the sea, as practiced at that time by the major powers. He was not overtly religious but respected the church of his childhood and took care to avoid desecrating churches along his route of plunder. The portrait artist Gil de Castro perhaps caught the vanity and vindicated feeling of redemption, particularly in the later painting.

Retired Argentine admiral and Bouchard biographer Miguel Angel DeMarco said in a 2018 interview,

> *"Yes, he is one of the most notable characters of the time of independence. He is a little subsumed by this Argentine custom of paying excessive...tribute to those who have the front row* [i.e, William Brown]. *"* [8]

In May 1982, a long-simmering dispute over sovereignty of an island group off the coast of Argentina came to a head. The islands called the Malvinas by Argentina were also claimed by Britain as the Falkland Islands. Argentine troops infiltrated the islands and raised their national flag on May 19th. Great Britain mobilized a large scale naval and ground force response. Out on the cold and stormy South Atlantic, the British submarine *HMS Conqueror* intercepted and fired three torpedoes at the Argentine cruiser *AR General Belgrano.* At least one of the torpedoes found its mark and sank the *Belgrano.* An errant torpedo also hit and slightly damaged the destroyer escort *AR Hipolito Bouchard*, a reconditioned United States destroyer, formerly *USS Borie*, which had seen action from World War II through Vietnam and had been sold to Argentina in 1977. This *Hipolito Bouchard* was just one of many ships named for their Argentine naval hero.

Over time, earthquakes crumbled the walls and ceiling of the Church of St. Javier, further sealing the memory of Bouchard. In 1952 the parish priest, Fr. Filberto Steux, came across the death certificate among old papers. In 1962, human remains deemed to be those of Hipolito Bouchard, based on the inscription *H.B. 1837* on the vault and later confirmed by the length of the bones, were removed from their underground tomb in the church at Nazca. His exhumed remains were paraded through Lima and Callao by six naval cadets before embarking on board a cruiser renamed *la Argentina,* which reprised parts of his epic voyage before finally mooring in the port of Buenos Aires. He received a hero's burial at the Naval Mausoleum at Cementerio de Chacarita in Buenos Aires with full military honors, and with the president of Argentina in attendance.[9.] Bouchard had at last returned to his adopted country. His name appears on streets, schools, buildings and monuments throughout Buenos Aires and the rest of Argentina. He is a revered hero in three South American nations and only William Brown has greater claim to the title "Father of the Argentine Navy." He is celebrated annually with the singing of the Argentine national anthem at his monument in his birthplace in Bormes-les-Mimosas as well as at St. Tropez, France. Less exuberant plaques and monuments mark the locations he came ashore in California in California's only pirate raid.

Christopher Columbus, who opened the New World as the 16th century dawned, may have said, *"You can never cross the ocean unless you have the courage to lose sight of the shore,"* Ignoring danger and death, Andre Paul "Hipolito" Bouchard crossed the oceans of the world and sailed into history, searching for a fat merchantman full of booty or an enemy warship to attack with a broadside in the name of liberty, a cause bigger than himself. *Corsario*!

Notes:

1. Charles C. Griffin, "Economic and Social Aspects of the Era of Spanish-American Independence, *Hispanic American Historical Review,* XXIX, 1949, in Lewis Hanke (ed.), *History of Latin American Civilization, vol. II, The Modern Age* (USA): Little, Brown & Co., 1967, p. 10.

2. Maria Arana, Bolivar. American Liberator, New York: Simon & Shuster, 2013, pp. 463-464.

3. John Lynch, San Martin. Argentine Soldier, American Hero, New Haven, CT: Yale University Press, 2009, p. 226.

4. Manuel Montt and Jose Francisco Gana, Address of the President of Chili July 28, 1857, forwarded by letter to Thomas Lord Cochrane in Thomas Cochrane, Narrative of Services in the Liberation of Chili, Peru and Brazil from Spanish and Portuguese Domination, 1858, A Public Domain Book, electronic edition, not paginated, 2012.

5. Thomas Cochrane, Letter of response to the President of Chili, November 5, 1857, Ibid.

6. Michael Kempe, Globalized Piracy and International Law 1500 – 1930, *Journal of Global History* (2010) 5, pp. 353-372, London School of Economics, pp. 353-372, https://d-nb.info, retrieved October 21, 2022.

7. Miguel Angel DeMarco, Bouchard: Halcon de los Mares. Corsario de la Libertad, Buenos Aires: Emece, 2018, (Spanish edition), pp. 229-230.

8. ____________, "Recien hace unos anos, un juez de EEUU absolvo a Bouchard de pirateria," interview with Claudia Peiro, *infobae,* October 10, 2018, http://www.infobae.com>2018/10/27. Retrieved September 14, 2022.

9. Robert Ulloa, "The End of Hipolito Bouchard," *Maritime Bulletin,* Institute of Historical-Maritime Studies of Peru – Maritime and Naval History, ed. Rosario Yika Uribe, February 27, 2018, https://boletinmaritimo.blogspot.com, retrieved Dec. 23, 2022.

Acknowledgements

To begin thanking all the people who helped bring this book to reality, let me give a nod of appreciation to all those whose kind reception to my earlier book, BADASS LAWMAN, gave me encouragement to pursue this project. And I would like to recognize those authors, both in North and South America, whose previous works about Hipolito Bouchard I respect and admire.

Special thanks to former faculty associate Gregorio Mora Torres Ph.D., Professor of Chicano-Chicana Studies at San Jose State University, who graciously wrote the foreword to this book. His conversation, critique and insights into the American wars of independence from Spain were brilliant and much appreciated.

Several longtime friends helped propel me forward. Friend since childhood Robert Izmirian guided me on all things nautical, and, along with Suzanne Smith, proved such marvelous hosts and enablers in my research foray to Santa Barbara. Together, their keen legal minds and eyes combed through the manuscript, ferreting out the early mistakes and calling me to task for fuzzy writing and fuzzier thinking.

Army buddy, financial guru and good friend Dan Kreer guided me to the historic locations in Monterey that appear in this book. When my own Spanish reading ability proved inadequate, my neighbor and dear friend Esther Corral-Carlson used her technology skills and Spanish language to help me access and translate some of the important materials in that language. Another former San Jose State colleague, Peter Young, now vice president of sponsored programs at Hawai'I Pacific University, ran interference for me with the museums and historical society in Hawai'i. *Mahalo ia oe.*

Among the research experts who provided guidance and source material were: Igor Polishehuk, Fort Ross Conservancy; James Perry, Executive Director Monterey County Historical

Society; Marsha Martin, Monterey Public Library; Jordan Leininger, Museum & Cultural Arts Division, City of Monterey; Gary Spradlin, Monterey History & Arts Association; Dez Alaniz, Archivist and Librarian, Santa Barbara Trust for Historic Preservation; Chris S. Ervin, Head Archivist and Adela Lisanti, Collections Manager, Santa Barbara Historical Museum; Chevon Vermeulen, Office Manager, San Juan Capistrano Historical Society; Cynthia Engle, Executive Director, Hawaiian Historical Society; staff at Museo Historico Nacional, Buenos Aires, Argentina; staff at Museo Naval de la Nacion, Buenos Aires, Argentina. Thank you all.

Thanks also to the staff of *Gallignani Livres Francais,* Paris, France, for helping me source English language material about Revolutionary France and the Napoleonic navy.

Once again, I'm deeply indebted to the creative skill of designer Briana Carlson Monaco and to Emily Veeh and her professional staff at Bookstand Publishing, an enjoyable association. As always, Brad Jones and Cindy Meister of Booksmart, Morgan Hill, have offered support for this local author.

Many pairs of eyes looked over parts, or all, of the manuscript in progress, searching out errors of fact or gremlins of style. If any mistakes or poor decisions in writing the narrative survived into publication, I alone take responsibility.

After months into researching and writing this story of Argentina, it was gratifying to see Argentina's dramatic win in the soccer World Cup. Congratulations to Lionel Messi, a modern-day Argentine national hero.

No one has a greater emotional investment in this book than my wife, Kathie, who endured my long hours at the keyboard or my far-away stare as I wrote silently inside my head at strange hours of the day or night. Her support and sharp pencil and love are invaluable and mean more than I can say.

Glossary of Ship Types and Nautical Terms

Types of Ships – Early 19th Century

Baltimore Clipper: Two masted schooner-like with square sails on foremast. Often used as blockade runner or privateer.

Barque: 3-5 masts, square rigged on all but aft-most mast

Barquentine 2-5 masts, only square rigged on foremast.

Boat: Any open small vessel for rowing or sailing.

Brig: Any variety of two mast, square rigged vessel.

Brigantine: 2 masts, square sails on foremast, fore-and-aft sails on main mast.

Clipper: Elegant square rigged merchant ship built for speed.

Corvette: Smallest of 3 mast, square rigged sailing warships. Also known as sloop of war or small frigate. 8-22 guns on a single deck.

Cutter: Fast, fore-and-aft rigged, single mast with double head sails. Used for patrol or smuggling. Up to 12 guns.

Dinghy: Small rowing or sailing boat, often a tender to a larger ship.

East Indiaman: Large, heavily armed European merchant ship for trade.

Felucca: Narrow, swift lateen (triangular sail) rigged sailing vessel, found on the Nile River and Mediterranean.

Frigate: 3 mast vessel with two full decks, 1 gun deck of 30-44 guns.

Galleon: Large square rigged, 3-4 mast vessel, such as Manila Galleons.

Longboat: Largest boat on board another, powered by oars or sail.

Lugger: Small ship, 1 or more lugger sails on 2-3 masts. 1-3 jibs on the bowsprit. Faster in coastal waters than square sailed ships but required larger crews. Used by smugglers, privateers.

Man O'War: A ship designed particularly as a warship.

Merchantman: A ship designed for trade.

Pirate: An armed ship indiscriminately plundering any other vessel. Or person.

Privateer: A private vessel raiding enemy shipping in wartime for the purpose of profit. A commissioned pirate.

Rating: British Admiralty rating for number of guns.

- First rate – warship with 100 or more guns on three decks.
- Second rate – 84-98 guns.
- Third rate – 64-80 guns.
- Fourth rate – 50-60 guns.
- Fifth rate – 32-44 guns.
- Sixth rate – 20-30 guns.

Schooner: Vessel with fore and aft sails on 2 or more masts, usually with 1-3 square sails on the foremast.

Ship: A sailing vessel with 3 or more square rigged masts (lower, top and topgallant) and a bowsprit.

Ship of the Line: Built to fight in line of battle, allowing each ship to fire full broadsides. Fourth rate or above, most commonly Third rate – 74 guns.

Sloop: Single mast, fore-and-aft rigged, also known as a cutter.

Sloop of war: Smallest 3 mast ship with 8-22 guns on a single deck. Also known as a corvette.

Tender: A vessel attending another vessel, for example ferrying sailors or supplies from ship to shore.

Whaler: A sturdy purpose-built ship with a large hold for processing whales.

Source: *Listing of Historical Sailing Ship Types and nomenclature.* http://www.ageofsail.met>aoshipty

Common Nautical Terms

Admiral: Senior naval officer of flag rank.

Aft: Toward the rear of a vessel.

Bow: Front of a vessel.

Cannister: Small iron balls packed in a case, fired from a cannon.

Carronade: Short cannon firing a heavy shot. Often mounted on a swivel as only gun on smaller ships.

Chain shot: Cannon balls linked by a chain to damage rigging and masts.

Commodore: Senior captain with overall command of a squadron.

Corsair (Fr.): Privateer (person or ship; see *Preface*).

Draft: Depth of the keel (bottom) below the waterline. Also, draught.

Ensign: Flag indicating nationality. Also, a junior officer.

Fathom: Measure of water depth equal to 6 feet.

First lieutenant: Officer second in command to the captain.

Flag officer: Senior officer directing a squadron.

Flagship: Vessel of a flag officer.

Fore-and-aft: Rigging parallel to the line of the ship.

Forward: Toward the front of a vessel.

Grapeshot: Small cast iron balls in a pouch fired at enemy personnel prior to boarding another ship.

Grappling hook: Iron claws attached to a rope thrown to pull ships together for boarding.

Jib: A sail forward of the mast.

Jibe: To change direction by turning the stern through the wind. The ship would be said to be "running before the wind." Also gybe (Br.).

Latitude: Measure of north-south location relative to the equator.

League: Measure of distance, three nautical miles.

Leeward: The side of a ship (or island) away from the direction of the wind. Or lee.

Longitude: Measure of east-west location relative to the prime meridian at Greenwich, England.

Mainsail: Large, triangular sail with a spar or boom to hold it open at bottom.

Marines: Soldiers serving aboard a ship.

Master: Captain of a commercial ship or senior warrant officer on a naval vessel.

Nautical mile: Equal to 1.5 land miles.

Pilot: An experienced navigator, especially at ports.

Port: 1. Left-hand side of a ship, facing forward. 2. The dock or terminus inside a harbor.

Powder magazine: Room in the ship's hull for storing gunpowder and ammunition.

Seaman: Generic term for sailor.

Starboard: Right-hand side of a vessel, facing forward.

Stern: Rear of a vessel.

Squadron: Small group of warships.

Square-rigged: Rigging perpendicular to the line of a ship, i.e., side to side.

Tack: To change direction by turning the bow through the wind. The ship would be said to be running "close-hauled." Also, the course of sailing.

Weigh: Raise the anchor from the sea floor.

Windward: The side of a ship (or island) facing the direction of wind.

Yard: Spar hung from mast from which a sail is hung.

Yard arm: Ends of the yard extending beyond the sail.

Selected Bibliography

Books

Amirell, Stefan Eklof, Pirates of Empire. Colonization and Maritime Violence in Southeast Asia, Cambridge: Cambridge University Press, 2019.

Anonymous, Colonial Argentina. The History of Argentina's Colonization and Struggle for Independence, Monee IL: Charles Rivers Editors, 2021.

Anonymous, History of California, Las Vegas, NV: Captivating History, 2022.

Altschull, J. Herbert, From Milton to McLuhan – The Ideas Behind American Journalism, New York: Longman, 1990.

Arana, Marie, Bolivar. American Liberator, New York: Simon & Schuster, 2013.

Barros Arana, Diego, General History of Chile, Books on Demand, 1889.

Benton, Lauren and Perl-Rosenthal, Nathan, eds., A World at Sea: Maritime Practices and Global History, Philadelphia: University of Pennsylvania Press, 2020.

Black, Jeremy, The French Revolutionary and Napoleonic Wars, Lanham MD: Rowman and Littlefield, 2022.

Buck, Peter H., Explorers of the Pacific: European and American Discoveries in Polynesia, Honolulu: Bishop's Museum, 1953.

Cairns, John C., France, Englewood Cliffs, NJ: Prentice-Hall Inc., 1965.

Castillo, Elias, A Cross of Thorns – The Enslavement of California's Indians by the Spanish Missions, Fresno CA: Craven Street Books, 2015.

Cochrane, Thomas Earl Dundonald, The Autobiography of a Seaman (1860), Lyons Press, electronic edition 2000.

_____________, Narrative of Services in the Liberation of Chili, Peru and Brazil from Spanish and Portuguese Domination, (1858), A Public Domain Book, electronic edition, 2012.

Cook, Todd, Pirates and Rogues of Monterey Bay, Charleston, SC: The History Press, 2019.

Corney, Peter, Voyages in the Northern Pacific, Honolulu, HI: Thos. G. Thrum, Publishers, 1896.

Dana, Richard Henry Jr., Two Years Before the Mast, originally published New York: Harper and Bros., 1840, kindle electronic edition – public domain, 2022.

De Marco, Miguel Angel, Bouchard: Halcon de los Mares. Corsario de la Libertad, Buenos Aires: Emece, 2018 (Spanish edition).

Faragher, John Mack, CALIFORNIA – An American History, New Haven, CT: Yale University Press, 2022.

Farris, Glenn J., (ed.) So Far from Home – Russians in Early California, Berkeley, CA: Heyday/University of Santa Clara, 2012.

Fernandez-Armesto, Felipe, Our America – A Hispanic History of the United States, New York: W.W. Norton, 2014.

Graffy, Neal, Historic Santa Barbara. An Illustrated History, San Antonio, TX: Historical Publishing Network, 2010.

Gibson, James R. and Istomin, Alexi A., Russian California 1806-1860, a History in Documents, vol. I, London: Haklyut Society, 2014.

____________, vol. II.

Green, Andrew, The History of Argentina, Monee, IL: self-published, 2022.

Hanke, Lewis (ed.), History of Latin American Civilization, vol. 2, The Modern Age, New York: Little Brown & Co. 1967.

Hobel, Robert, The Philippines, Hong Kong: Robert Rovera Ltd., 1990.

Hoffmann, Stanley et. al., In Search of France, New York: Harper & Row, 1963.

Hunt, Lynn and Censer, Jack R., The French Revolution and Napoleon, London: Bloomsbury Academic, 2022.

Johnson, Lyman L., Workshop of the Revolution. Plebeian Buenos Aires and the Atlantic World 1776-1810, Durham, NC: Duke University Press, 2011.

Kilmeade, Brian and Yearger, Dan, Thomas Jefferson and the Tripoli Pirates, New York: Sentinel, 2015.

Lynch, John, San Martin-Argentine Soldier, American Hero, New Haven, CT: Yale University Press, 2009.

Mathes, W. Michael, (ed.), The Russian-Mexican Frontier: Mexican Documents Regarding the Russian Establishment in California 1808-1842, Jenner, CA: Fort Ross Interpretive Association, 2008.

Matsuda, Mark K., Pacific Worlds. A History of Seas, Peoples and Cultures, Cambridge: Cambridge University Press, 2012.

Matthews, Owen, Glorious Misadventures – Nikolai Rezanov and the Dream of a Russian America, New York: Bloomsbury, 2013.

McLaughlin, David J., Soldiers, Scoundrels, Priests: Stories of the Men and Women Behind the Missions of California, Scottsdale, AZ: Pentacle Press, 2004.

Melzer, Michael. The Patriot Pirate, Pasadena CA: Scoop, 2016.

Markham, Sir Clements R., The Story of Majorca and Minorca, London: Smith, Elder & Co., 1908.

Mora-Torres, Gregorio (trans./ed.) Californio Voices – The Oral Memoirs of Jose Maria Amador and Louisa Asisara, Denton TX: University of North Texas Press, 2005.

Morrison, Samuel Eliot, John Paul Jones – A Sailor's Biography, Boston: Little Brown & Co., 1959.

Resendez, Andres, A Land So Strange – The Epic Tale of Cabeza de Vaca, New York: Basic Books, 2007.

Saunt, Claudio, West of the Revolution – An Uncommon History of 1776, New York: W.W.Norton, 2014.

Spaulding, Edward Selden, A Brief Story of Santa Barbara, Santa Barbara Historical Society, Santa Barbara, CA: Pacific Coast Publishing Co., 1964.

Taylor, Stephen, Commander – The Life and Exploits of Britain's Greatest Frigate Captain, New York: W.W. Norton & Co., 2012.

Uhrowczik, Peter, The Burning of Monterey – The 1818 Attack on California by the Privateer Bouchard, Los Gatos, CA: Cyril Books, 2001.

Wright, Gordon, France in Modern Times-1760 to the Present, Chicago: Rand McNally & Co., 1966.

Winchester, Simon, Pacific, New York, Harper Collins, 2015.

Articles, Journals and Online Sources

Alexander, William DeWitt, "Captain Bouchard and the Spanish Pirates," *The Friend,* vol. 49, no. 3, Honolulu, HI, March 1891.

Annen, Dominic. "Tricolor and Union Jack at Sea: How the French Revolution Decapitated Napoleon's Navy and Thereby Ruined His Ambitions," (2015) *Student theses, Papers and Projects (History).43,* https://digitalcommons.wou.edu/his/43.

Anonymous, "The Siege and the Taking of Malta," https://www.napoleon.org.

__________, "Maltese History and Heritage," https://vassallohistory.word press.com>french- blockade.

__________, "Capture of the Genereux 18th February 1800," *Three Decks,* https://www.threedecks.org.

__________, "How a Band of Franciscan Friars Kept the Russians out of California," St. Francis and the Americas Project, Arizona State University, https://stfrancis.clas.asu.edu>article.

__________, "The Militia of the Sea," https://www.battlefields.org>learn>articles>militia-sea.

__________, "Pirates, Privateers, Corsairs, Buccaneers: What's the Difference?" https://www.britannica.com>story.

___________, "Brown's Corsair Expedition to the Pacific," ed. Nov. 26, 2020, https://secondwiki>wiki>ecpedicic3b3n-corsaria-de, Retrieved August 10, 2022.

__________, "Almirante William Brown," History of Ireland, ,https://www.historyireland.com>almirante-william-brown, Retrieved July 9, 2022.

___________, "Santa Barbara Mission – Early History of the California Coast," https://www.nps.gov.>travel.

___________, "The Cast Iron Castaway," The Bowers Blog. April 27, 2017, https://www.bowers.org>collection>collection-blog, retrieved Jan. 5, 2023.

Bealer, Lewis W., "Bouchard in the Islands of the Pacific," *Pacific Historical Review,* vol. 4, no. 4, Dec. 1935.

Bowen, Andy, "The Story of Le Genereux – a tale of escapes, captures and tenuous celebrity connections," July 19, 2017, https://nelsonandnorfolk.wordpress.com.

Buchanan, Shirley Elaine, "HE KAMI INITINI; How Native Hawaiian Governance and American Indian Policy Became Linked in the Nineteenth Century," Ph.D. dissertation, University of Hawai'I, Manoa, 2019.

Burgess, Sherwood D., "Pirate or Patriot? Hypolite Bouchard and the Invasion of Monterey," *The American West,* vol. xi, no. 6, November 1974.

Burns, Peter, "How Russia Almost Owned a Big Piece of California," *The Bold Italic,* October 11, 2020. https://thebolditalic.com.

Campbell, Leon G., "The Spanish Presidio in Alta California During the Mission Period," J*ournal of the West,* vol. 16, no. 4, October 1977.

Caputo, Sara, "Mercenary gentlemen? The transnational service of foreign quarterdeck officers in the Royal Navy of the American and French Wars, 1775 – 1815," *Historical Research,* vol. 94, issue 266, November 2021, pp. 806-26. https://doi.org/10.1093/hisres/htab028.

Cerecedo, Carlos, "Hipolito Bouchard. Pirate or Patriot?" *La Campana,* The Santa Barbara Trust for Historical Preservation, Winter Cochrane, 1995-96.

DeMarco, Miguel Angel, "Recien hace unos anos, un juez de EEUU absolve a Bouchard de pirateria," interview with Claudia Peiro, *infobae*, Oct. 27, 2018, (in Spanish) http://www.infobae.com>2018/10/27.

Diaz-Flores, Gerardo, "What is the Difference Between Corsairs and Pirates?" *Relatos e Hiastorias en Mexico*, no. 118 https://relatosehistorias enmex.translategoog/la-coleccion/118-piratas? (Spanish).

Dolin, Eric Jay, "American Rebels at Sea," *American Heritage,* vol. 67, no. 3, Summer 2022.

Frayler, John, "Privateers in the American Revolution," National Park Service, https://www.nps.gov>articles.

Girard, Philippe R., "The Ugly Duckling: The French Navy and the Saint-Domingue Expedition, 1801-1803," *International Journal of Naval History,* December 1, 2010.

Kempe, Michael, "Globalized Piracy and International Law. 1500 – 1930," *Journal of Global History* 5 (2010), London School of Economics. https://d-nb.nfo,

Lawler, Andrew, "Did Francis Drake Really Land in California?" *Smithsonian Magazine,* September 26, 2019, https://www.smithsonianmag.com>history.

Martinez Shaw, Carlos and Alfonso Mola, Marina, "The Philippine Islands: A vital crossroads during the first globalization period,"

Culture and History Digital Journal, 3(1) e004, May 15, 2014, https://cutureandhistory.revistas.csic.ed>article.

Morris, Susan L., et. al., "Murder, Massacre, and Mayhem on the California Coast, 1814-1815: Newly Translated Russian American Company Documents Reveal Company Concern Over Violent Clashes," *Journal of California and Great Basin Anthropology,* vol. 34, no. 1, 2014, https://www.nps.gov.>subjects>upload>JCGBA.

Morrison, S.E., "Boston Traders in the Hawaiian Islands 1789-1823," *The Washington Historical Quarterly*, vol. 12, no. 3, July 1921, https://journals.lib.washington.edu, retrieved Aug. 31, 2022.

Plunkett, Eric, "The Saga of Orange County's Pirates," San Juan Capistrano Visitor Series., part 8, October 28, 2018, *Visions of California* blog. https:// visions of California blogspot.com>2018, retrieved Sept. 10, 2022.

Porter, Catherine; Meheut, Constant; Apuzzo, Matt, and Gebrekidan, Selam, "The Ransom. The Root of Haiti's Misery: Reparations to Enslavers," originally published as "A Land of Riches, but Not for its Own People," *New York Times,* May 22, 2022.

Ulloa, Roberto, "The End of Hipolito Bouchard," *Maritime Bulletin, Institute of Historical-Maritime Studies of Peru-Maritime and Naval History,* ed. Rosario Yika Uribe, February 27, 2018, https://bolrtinmaritimo.logspot.com.

Watrous, Stephen, "Russian Expansion to America," *Fort Ross*, Fort Ross Conservancy, 1998. https://www.fortross.org>russian-american-company.

Manuscripts, Letters, and Archival Material

Anonymous, *History of the State of California and Biographical Record of Santa Cruz, San Benito, Monterey and San Luis Obispo Counties*, Chicago: Chapman Publishing Co., 1903

Bouchard, Hipolito, *"The Recognition of Don Edward Butler as Agent of the Government of the Upper Provinces,"* 11 Sept. 1818, Hawaii State Archives, Foreign Office and Executive Records 1790-1900, Box 402-2-9, Chronological file 1790-1849.

___________, *Manuscripo de Bouchard, 1819,* Archivo General de la Nacion, Gobierno Nacional 1810-1828, War. Naval Campaigns, V-XXIV-11-6, Buenos Aires.

"El Corso con Brown en el Pacifico," Comision Nacional de Homenaje al Capitan De Navio Hipolito Bouchard, Argentina, 1967.

Lydecker, Robert C., "The Archives of Hawaii, *Papers of the Hawaiian Historical Society*, no. 13, Honolulu, Territory of Hawaii, 1906, http://hdl.handle.net/10524/979, retrieved Aug. 27, 2022

Malcolm, Barrie Earl, "The Soldiers of Spain's California Army, 1769-1821," *Dissertations and Theses.* Paper 4690. M.A. Thesis, Portland State University, 1993, https://doi.org/10.15760/etd.6574.

Oak, Henry Lebbeus, Annals of the Spanish Northwest: California 1840-45, (San Francisco?): vol. 4, 1886, facsimilie edition Kessinger Publishing, 2010.

Piriz, Jose Maria, Manuscript, 1819, Archivo Museo Mitre, Armario 1, Cajon 11, Carpeta 6, Documento 1, Buenos Aires.

Shur, Leonid (ed.), *"The Khlebnikov Archive, Unpublished Journal (1800-1837) and Travel Notes*," University of Alaska Press (John Bisk, trans.).

Sola, Pablo Vicente de, *Report of Pablo Vicente de Sola, Governor, to the Viceroy of New Spain, Don Juan Ruiz de Apadeca*, December 12, 1818.

Yanovsky, Governor, "*Secret Instructions from Governor Yanovsky to Agent Khlebnikov about a Voyage to Alta California in the Brig Il'mena*," 1 no. 11, New Archangel. May 31, 1820, in Gibson, James R., Istomin, Alexei A. and Tishkov, Valery A., Russian California 1806-1860 A History in Documents, vol. 1, London: The Hakluyt Society, 2014.

Newspapers

Barratt, Elizabeth, "When Argentina's Flag Flew Over Monterey," *Alta Vista Magazine, Monterey Herald,* Nov. 21, 1993.

Baserga, Horacio, Letter to the editor, *Monterey Peninsula Herald,* Nov. 7, 1964.

Book B of Deeds (1835) in *Gilroy Advocate,* July 31, 1869.

Bullrich, Conrado, Etchebarne, "Cuando Hawai'I tuvo bandera Argentina," *La Nacion* (Argentina), sec. 7, p. 5, 14 Sept. 1997.

Siegel, Jan, "Don Juan Avila Recounts the Pillaging of Capistrano," *Capistrano Dispatch*, April 13-26, 2012, p. 24.

Miscellaneous

Geni, genealogical data base.

Family Search.org, genealogical data base.

Ancestry.com, genealogical database.

"The Artists and Their Artwork," brochure, Santa Barbara County Courthouse Docent Council.

Map and Guide to Mission San Juan Capistrano, www.missionsjc.com.

"Times of Revolution," Buenos Aires, Ministerio de Cultura, Argentina, https://museohistoriconational.cultura.gob.ar.

www.ingramcontent.com/pod-product-compliance
Lightning Source LLC
Chambersburg PA
CBHW071325120626
46546CB00002B/443

* 9 7 8 1 9 5 6 7 8 5 3 8 8 *